FLY FISHING FOR GRAYLING

Previous books by the author:

The Grayling Angler, 1982, H.F. & G. Witherby

The New Illustrated Dictionary of Trout Flies, 1986, Allen & Unwin, 1988, Unwin Hyman, 1991, Collins

To Rise A Trout, 1988, Crowood Press, Revised 1994

A Guide to River Trout Flies, 1989, 1995, Crowood Press

Trout on a Nymph, 1990, Crowood Press

The World's Best Trout Flies, 1994, Boxtree, 1995, Tiger Books

Collins Illustrated Dictionary of Trout Flies, 1995

FLY FISHING FOR GRAYLING

JOHN ROBERTS

EXCELLENT PRESS
LUDLOW

First Published 1999 by Excellent Press
7 Corve Street
Ludlow
Shropshire SY8 1DB

This edition is limited to 1250 copies signed by the author.

274

A copy of the British Library cataloguing in Publication Data for this title is available from the British Library.

ISBN 1900318 11 3
Printed in Great Britain by
TJ International Ltd

Contents

Photography Credits

E.T. Atkinson	plate (i)
Rod Calbrade	plate (iii) b
Malcolm Greenhalgh	plate (ii) b
Terry Griffiths	plate (ix), (x), (xi), (xii)
Lars-Åke Olsson	plate (ii) a
Michel Roggo	plates (v), (vi) (vii)
Roy Shaw	plate (viii) a

The remainder were taken by the author.

Dedication

In memory of David Howden 1953–1998,
lifelong friend and fishing companion

Acknowledgements

I AM INDEBTED TO a number of people who have willingly shared their greater wisdom of various grayling matters. First, and to whom much is owed are Paul Marriner, Lars-Åke Olsson and Oliver Edwards, each a good friend whose opinion and advice I value. They read and commented on a draft or sections of this book. But for them my errors would be more liberally dispersed. I am grateful too to Bernard Benson, dry-fly fisherman of extraordinary skill and equally dry wit, for allowing me to pick his brains; Dr Ron Broughton for permission to quote from his writing; Stuart Crofts for advice about stonefly behaviour; Oliver Edwards for many of the superbly-tied flies that grace this book, for access to a length of the Wharfe with big grayling, and for permission to quote from his writing; Ross Gardiner, the Scientific Officer of the Grayling Society for his generosity in providing data and information about many aspects of grayling growth rates and lifecycle; Hans van Klinken for his friendship, advice and for *the* fly; Dr Jurek Kowalski for his expert tuition on the Polish and Czech nymph methods, and for commenting and correcting the relevant text; Leon Links for his encouragement and supply of good ideas; David Liversedge for his assistance in compiling the original list of grayling rivers; Dr Hugo Martel for advice on Continental grayling flies; Mike Mee who suffers my company each year on the Avon and Wylye; Robin Mulholland OBE, Chairman of the

Grayling Society and generous fishing host, for permission to quote from his writing; Arthur Oglesby for that first grayling; Dr Vincent Piriou for advice on French grayling flies; Roy Shaw, good friend and frequent companion on the West Beck; Thomas Stevens for advice on grayling optics; Sidney Vines for information on Frank Sawyer; Dr John Woolland for permission to quote from his published research. In addition I would like to thank J. Bryant, John Davison, R.A.'Taff' Stevens for recommending grayling patterns.

The flies in the colour plates were tied by their creators: Simon Ashworth, Theo Bakelaar, Oliver Edwards, Marjan Fratnik, Hans van Klinken, Jurek Kowalski, Leon Links, Roman Moser, Lars-Åke Olsson, Adam Sikora, Robert Spiller, Juha Vainio, Mike Weaver, John Woods; additional flies were tied by Oliver Edwards, John Woods, the author and Crystal River products.

1

GRAYLING: A PERSONAL VIEW

SEVENTEEN YEARS IS RATHER a long time between the first and second editions of a book. Viewed in the light of sales of best-selling fiction the mere two thousand, three hundred and twenty one copies of *The Grayling Angler* which took the best part of eight years to sell is hardly a figure to have publishers courting the author with champagne lunches. Had any publisher other than Tony Witherby invested his time and capital in the book it would have been remaindered within a couple of years of publication. But Tony was not from the usual publishing mould with an eye merely to a quick profit or a place in the sales charts. He cared deeply about his books and if he believed in a book he would stick with it to the end. Tony Witherby may have been quirky in his choice of the tiny handful of books he published but certainly he could also pick some winners. Who else would have backed Hugh Falkus's book on the obscure branch of sea-trout fishing in 1962?

I remember being horrified at the price of £8.50 for *The Grayling Angler* when it was published in 1982. However, I will be happy today to refund the money to any dissatisfied buyer. At least the book has proved a good investment for anyone unhappy with its contents. My fear was whether a book from an unknown author would be accepted. I was anxious for a good review and concerned about what established authors might say. Fortunately, it found favour with Donald Overfield in *Trout and Salmon*, and Sidney Vines in *The Field* was kind enough to suggest that the author 'has produced an admirable book and we shall hear more from him.' I have forever been grateful to both reviewers for easing my doubts. It is quite probable that without this encouragement I would not have considered writing further books. In the intervening years scores of grayling anglers have written to me or have spoken kindly about the book, many wanting to know where to buy a copy. I have been encouraged to think that my second grayling book, loosely based on the first edition, could be justified.

Writing for publication lays oneself open to criticism of what one writes or the way it is written. I have been fortunate in finding agreement and encouragement from many sources. Perhaps the most satisfying aspect of writing is that I have made a lot of friends through writing *The Grayling Angler* and subsequent books. The first edition of this book was the key to a very much wider, a world-wide fishing experience and the spark to new friendships across continents. Writing the book proved highly productive; it was the catalyst to so many new fishing opportunities and to meeting some marvellous people and expert anglers.

For this much revised volume I have omitted the chapters on bait fishing, the gourmet's grayling and grayling in print, and rewritten and expanded the more important sections on fly fishing methods where the real changes have been taking place. The rest of the text has been almost entirely rewritten in the light of nearly two decades of further experience.

Over the last twenty years there has been a considerable increase of interest in grayling fishing both in the U.K. and in the rest of Europe where grayling are found. The fourfold growth of the Grayling Society from about three hundred members in 1982 to twelve hundred today indicates its wider popularity. When writing the first edition of the book I had not fished beyond these shores and this was reflected in my parochial approach. Now with experience of Lapland, Continental Europe and North America I feel better qualified to write from wider experience. Generally speaking, grayling are more fully appreciated elsewhere in Europe where on many rivers they are the principal game fish without having to be second best to trout. It is significant that three European developments have had a major, very considerable influence in the way we have changed our fishing for grayling since the early 1980s. British and Continental fly fishing for grayling has changed irrevocably through the influence of bead-head flies popularised originally by Roman Moser, the creation of the best fast water fly on the planet, the Klinkhamer Special from Hans van Klinken, and the deep, short line nymph techniques of Eastern Europe. If only for these three changes in our grayling fishing, a revision of my book is required. Sadly, not since Frank Sawyer have British grayling fishers contributed very much that is new. These three developments, all devised for grayling, have also radically altered the way we fish for trout. I am delighted that grayling anglers have been the innovators in river trout fishing these last two decades. The species that was once scorned by so many trout fishers is the source of inspiration of much that is new in river fly fishing.

I rarely bait fish for grayling now. There was a time when it would have been my preferred method from November onwards. Today I enjoy fly fishing and the challenge it presents far more and the only occasions in recent years I have been found with a trotting rod is in the company of one of my sons or their friends, fulfilling a promise of an introduction to grayling. On the northern rivers and streams where I used maggots or brandlings they were an easy option. With luck, grayling could be caught almost whatever the weather and irrespective of the water conditions. It was always possible for a bait to be presented somewhere where grayling would take it. Blank days were extremely rare, even in very poor conditions. In ideal conditions, the fishing was just too easy. After three minutes tuition, someone who has never held a fishing rod may catch a lot of grayling; I doubt if the same is true of fly fishing. My reluctance to use worm or maggot also stems, in part, from my increased commitment to grayling as a game fish. I would rather not fish for them with coarse fishing methods. I would never deny anyone else the right to chose to use bait, especially on rivers where there is a long tradition, but my strong preference is for the fly.

A few anglers mix the two fishing styles and use a heavily weighted bug pattern below a float. When Richard Walker suggested this in the 1970s I tried it with modest success but I had not heard of its use very much until recently. I understand today that the practice is quite common on Scottish rivers where very large bugs or caseless caddis patterns produce good catches.

One day I may go back to the trotting rod, especially if I want a complete change in the way I fish. I may also be drawn back out of sheer frustration. I write these words at the beginning of March after an infuriating

February's fishing; three days, one grayling. I find there is no more difficult fly fishing than grayling fishing in February; the nomadic shoals, the weather and water conditions, their reduced feeding, too often conspire against me. I confess that on the Yorkshire Dales' rivers I often find the February shoals very hard to find, and even when I'm convinced that I must be fishing over grayling, they may not co-operate. I have little doubt that the more certain way to catch grayling from mid-November onwards is on bait.

I was fortunate enough to be born in York[1], at the centre of a county that leaves the rest of the country in its wake when it comes to producing the very best and widest range of grayling fishing. It was left to three Yorkshiremen of the nineteenth century, Jackson, Pritt[2] and Walbran, to bring to the fore the fact that grayling fishing was also a fly fisherman's sport and that grayling were every bit as game and sporting a fish as trout. Today, all over the country, trout fishers extend their fly fishing season by pursuing the fish that has been appreciated by northerners for centuries. Even in the last twenty years there has been a noticeable increase in the number of grayling anglers, in the promotion of the species in journals, and in the attitude of other fly fishermen. Most fly fishers I meet who do not fish for grayling do not because they live so far from grayling rivers. They would love to fish for grayling if they had ready access to them.

Over the years the much maligned grayling has been cursed and blasphemed, slandered and libelled by those who have failed to recognise a truly game fish, which far from being discounted as worthless to the fly fisher should be regarded at least on a par with its riverbed-fellow, the trout. Grayling fishing ranks below trout fishing in its expense only. Game fishermen are becoming aware of the ever increasing costs of a season's trout fishing and if grayling fishing is permitted in the price of a season's trout ticket, the value is doubled. The autumn and winter months may be spent pursuing a fish that will challenge and reward even the most demanding of fishermen.

[1] Grayling remains from between the first and twelfth centuries have been found in archaeological deposits in the York area. Can anywhere else in Britain claim such a tradition? Source: Jones, A.K.G. (1988) *The Exploitation of Wetlands. Symposia for the Association of Environmental Archaeology* No.7

[2] T.E. Pritt was born in Lancashire but lived for most of his life in his adopted Yorkshire

Traditionally, the grayling fishing season has followed on after the end of the trout season. Attention turned from one species to another. The earliest legal date when grayling can be caught in England and Wales is June 16th, midsummer and fourteen weeks before the traditional start to the season. On all the northern rivers I fish grayling have recovered from spawning long before mid-June and few of the grayling I catch unintentionally when trout fishing in April and May show signs of being unfit.I have come to regard the opening day of the grayling season as June 16th and I will fish for them with appropriate flies and methods from then on. I cannot speak for grayling in the southern chalk streams where my summer grayling experience is nil and where I suspect summer grayling may not be fully recovered for another month, but the last twenty-five years fishing in the rest of the country and in Europe indicates that summer grayling are every bit as sporting as those of autumn. Elsewhere in Europe there is no artificially introduced delay; grayling are valued so highly that when the official season starts so do anglers. Why wait ? On most rivers grayling are fully fit by early summer and I fish for them alongside trout with the same enthusiasm I once reserved for grayling in October. On October 1st my grayling fishing continues; the season has not just begun. Doing so gives me much more scope for fly fishing in the second half of the summer and provides opportunities for different fishing methods for summer grayling from those usually required in autumn and winter. Low summer water levels, warm weather dusk fishing, the greater range of aquatic and terrestrial flies mean a much broader approach to grayling fishing than the methods and patterns required for October and beyond. I make no bones about it, I regard grayling fishing every bit as highly as trout fishing (I guarantee every fish will be wild; there are few places where that will be so for trout), so I do not inhibit or unnecessarily delay my fishing for them. They should never be merely an appendage to the trout season.

My first grayling was caught one bleak November day on the River Nidd above Harrogate. A watery sun had barely penetrated the heavy cloud, with insufficient strength to warm what little of my skin was left exposed. It was not the most suitable day to be outside, nor to be wading an ice cold river. That bitterly cold afternoon's fishing was the result of a month or so's constant nagging at Arthur Oglesby to take me, as he had promised, trotting for grayling.

In my childhood I had fished with little success, catching a few roach and eels on some very old tackle. Alas, I had no Mr Crabtree[3] at my shoulder. Failure led to disillusionment, and at about 13 years of age, when my one and only reel dropped into twelve feet of water, I decided to call it a day and parted with the rest of my tackle. It was not until my early twenties that friends persuaded me to give it another chance. Arthur was doing his best to wean me away from the couple of seasons of coarse fishing that I had behind me, and to point me well on the way to becoming a game fisherman. The transition (not that he had planned it this way) was to be in two stages. First, the game quarry by coarse methods, and finally, game quarry by game fishing methods. The first stage was how I came to be nearly freezing to death that November afternoon up to my thighs in icy water in a pair of borrowed waders. I believe I caught three or four grayling by trotting a maggot down some deep glides and I remember quite clearly missing dozens of takes as the float dipped for a split second, and I struck an eternity too late. They were particularly shy that day and far from sympathetic towards a novice. The afternoon was not spectacular, the grayling were thin lean ten-inch fish, and Arthur has long forgotten the day, but my first grayling is indelibly etched in my memory. Most game fishers would rather remember their first trout or salmon on the fly – but that grayling will remain a milestone with me.

In the years that followed, the summers were spent fly fishing for trout, the metamorphosis from coarse to game fisherman complete. The autumns and winters were dedicated to pursuing with fly and bait the fish that has become my number one quarry. Francis Francis, when he first called the grayling 'The Lady of the Stream' chose an apt title; for five months a year she becomes my mistress, my sole source of piscatorial

[3] In 1993 I was to enjoy a dinner with Bernard Venables, author of the Mr Crabtree books, with a dozen other Grayling Society members. Finally meeting one of one's boyhood heroes could have proved very disappointing; this certainly was not. Tens of thousands of anglers of my generation were inspired by his writing and drawing. I wanted to tell him exactly how we had felt as ten-year old boys, imagining what Mr Crabtree would do in a situation we found ourselves in, and how he had filled our dreams with hope. He listened patiently as I told my story. I must have briefly thought that I was unique to have fallen under his spell thirty years ago, but it dawned on me that he had heard it all before, a thousand times, from every middle-aged angler he had met. Small of stature, but a great man to so many, in his eighties he had lost none of his interest in fishing. He was no fallen idol but a witty, sprightly, well informed and cultured hero

pleasure, demanding of me more time than a married man should fairly give to his hobbies, and often testing the patience of a forgiving and lenient wife.

The epithet 'Lady of the Stream' has remained with the grayling. Frank Sawyer wrote 'By some, grayling are considered to be the lady of the chalk streams – perhaps so, but I think a very greedy lady and a flirt.' He was nearer the mark for sometimes she is less the lady and more the trollop, ever willing to please all those who seek her favours. Sawyer went on with his analogy, describing grayling as 'nicely shaped and good to look at'. I agree so far as his comments extend to the fish but some might find his depiction a little too sexist today.

There is some debate as to whether the overall national grayling stocks are deteriorating, remaining constant, or actually increasing. On some rivers the latter claim may be upheld, where angling clubs or a water authority have seen fit to improve a fishery by introducing the species into previously unstocked water. In some rivers the number of fish has remained a constant level for many years, angling practice, fishery management and mother nature have found a balance. I fear the third category is the one most likely to be growing, where stocks are actually decreasing. This is largely due to pressure from two sources.

The first pressure is from trout fishers who seek to promote an exclusively 'trout only' water. F.M. Halford in the 1880s was aware of the same problem and wrote of the overheard conversation of two trout fishers wishing that the last pike in the River Test might be choked in the act of swallowing the last grayling. Sadly this attitude is still voiced on some fisheries over a century later. One of the better managed clubs which shows a much more enlightened attitude towards grayling is the Piscatorial Society[4]. They enjoy fishing some excellent water on the Wiltshire Avon and the Wylye. After years of electrofishing the grayling they discovered this method had severe limitations and implications. The electrodes missed the grayling in their first year of growth and these went on to thrive because of the reduced competition. The result was a much larger 1+ class the following year. The grayling removal was counter-productive. Coupled with the results of research[5] that suggested that competition

[4] *The Journal of the Grayling Society* Autumn 1992. Article by Robin Mulholland

[5] Dr Graham Bellamy *Competition between trout and grayling on the River Lambourne* , PhD thesis, Reading University

between trout and grayling in chalk streams is very limited and that the best way to improve trout populations is to improve their habitat, they opted for a change in policy. For the last ten years grayling have been left alone and the river has found its own balance of excellent trout and grayling fishing. The latter thrive at all ages and both continue to do well through habitat improvement.

My criticism lies with those fishery and club managements who will not tolerate the presence of grayling, believing that every possible lie and pool will be infested with them, depriving trout of food and hindering the growth of stocks and the growth of individual fish. Over recent years there has been an enlightenment in management minds and the situation is much improved. In an unstocked river fished mainly for trout there is fair reason to keep grayling in control so that the quality of trout fishing is maintained. But I suggest that this should begin by first trying to improve trout habitat rather than by eliminating the grayling. The trout/grayling balance can be controlled to provide autumn and winter grayling fishing and good spring and summer trout fishing.

In water stocked with trout, the very fact that carnivorous fish of the 3+ age are artificially kept at a high level – the loss mainly due to successful angling – ensures that they are the dominant species and the grayling are kept in control. I have not come across a trout-stocked water where grayling have gained the upper hand. In some years grayling are prolific spawners and in others the reverse is true (this variation appears to be more marked than the trout's). Consequently stocks rise and fall from season to season. No matter how favourable the spawning environment has been for the trout, their stocks are artificially maintained at a level necessary for good fishing.

The second reason for the deterioration of stock lies with grayling fishers. When I wrote *The Grayling Angler* I suggested there was then a comparative scarcity of two pound grayling when compared with twenty years previously and that this and the less frequent large catches from once prolific rivers was due to some years of killing too many fish. It was commonplace then to kill thirty or forty fish and to return none at all. Clearly, such a continued practice by significant numbers of anglers could not be maintained. Few today would be so inconsiderate as to kill such a number. In general terms, my experience and that of anglers I meet on the riverside is that the quality of grayling fishing has improved in the last twenty years. There will be exceptions to this rule where pollution has ruined a river or where in isolated ignorance a fishery management has over-stocked with trout, but overall I believe the picture is improving. I am also hopeful that the greater dissatisfaction of anglers catching too many stocked trout and fewer wild ones is leading to an easing back of stocking in rivers. This can only be to the benefit of the indigenous wild trout and grayling.

Although we sometimes look with envy at grayling fishing in Scandinavia and elsewhere in Europe, not all their fisheries are well run nor are their angling practices always very far sighted. For some years my Swedish friend, Lars-Åke Olsson has controlled the Idsjostrommen, part of the River Gim in mid-Sweden. Before he took control of the water anglers were permitted to kill any number of takeable grayling and trout. The fishing had deteriorated to a low level. Lars introduced a no-kill policy, improved the habitat, restricted the rods on the water and permitted only fly fishing. A decade later, his water is gaining an international reputation, with scientific surveys of the water confirming a five hundred percent increase in the number of grayling. Within the first month of the most recent season twenty grayling between twenty and twenty-three inches were caught. The fishing at Gimdalen is a fine example what can be done by a combination of good river management and educating angling attitudes.

One cannot be too dogmatic about fishing, least of all about grayling fishing. Their varying location in the river, from hugging the bottom of the deepest pools, to holding in a mere few inches of fast riffle water, requires a very adaptable approach and an open mind before one starts the day's fishing. Their mid-winter preference for the deep river bed may change within minutes to a willingness to rise to the dry fly even after the turn of the year, thus there are few rules to follow except that of flexibility.

I doubt if the grayling can be surpassed for the numbers of fish that can be regularly caught at one session and for the battle they put up on appropriate tackle. No other winter fish of its weight puts up the resistance of these spirited fighters. The reason why there are an increasing number of grayling fishers is simply that the result justifies the effort that goes into catching them. Whether one is fortunate to fish with a sedge pupa in the twilight of a summer's evening, a dry fly during the mild days of autumn or with a worm from the snow covered riverbanks of February, the rewards are the same; a prospective catch of fish that will stimulate, entertain and satisfy that part of our make-up that makes every fisherman head towards water.

What is written in the following pages is devoted to considering how to catch grayling, and is not an anthology dedicated to gilded autumnal days. It is left to the poets to expound how man responds to nature and to the fisherman to catch fish. In the quest for grayling one will enjoy the exhilaration of fishing amidst autumn's splendours and I hope the countryside will be as rewarding as the day's fishing. Summer days fishing in the Arctic tundra, Austrian mountains or rolling Slovenian meadows are unforgettable for the visiting grayling fisher. Perhaps most writers have overdone it a little; they have failed to mention the wind and rain, snow and fog of the traditional British grayling season. The true grayling devotee will be out in all weather in the hope of a memorable fishing day. Days that have warranted a gold star in the fishing diary have been those when notable fish have been caught and not because of the fine weather or beautiful scenery. It is towards more gold star days that this book is written, when the tug, tug, tug of a big grayling hooked in a deep pool, or the corkscrewing, gyrating figure-of-eight struggle of the smaller fish has been felt again and again, when the Lady of the Stream has been a little too reckless for her own good.

2

The Facts of Life

Habitat, Distribution and Lifecycle

'Probably it was in that moment that all the bickering and back-talk of husbands and wives originated; when Adam called to Eve to come and look at his first fish while it was still silver and vivid in its living colours; and Eve answered she was busy.'

Christopher Morley, *Mince Pie*

'Trout may be called handsome – grayling are a beautiful fish.'

E. Marshall-Hardy

WITHOUT DOUBT THE FEMININE description of the grayling applies; it is truly a fish of beauty. The stubborn ugliness of the carp, the predatory viciousness of the pike, the majestic sheen of the salmon, the handsome sombre coat of the brown trout, serve only to emphasise the beauty of the grayling. The glittering hues sparkle in the autumn sun, reflecting the variety and spectrum of colour found in its kaleidoscopic brilliance and richness of its complexion. Just what the subtler colours consist of seems to vary from river to river, and grayling writers of the past have found it hard to agree upon a common description of its colouring. Across Europe there are definite regional or national differences in the fin colouring and in the body spots. Its large dorsal fin is one of the species' most distinguishing features. In the past British writers have variously described it as:

> 'purplish bands and ocelli which have a purplish red centre … and some black spots'.
>
> 'Scarlet spots and wavy lines upon a lighter background of reddish-brown'.
>
> 'Short red and black bars on a lighter background – being comparable to the wing of a butterfly'.

Trevor Housby depicted the fish most vividly: 'A knight's banner of a fin. Waving tartan red in the stream, and a chain mail coat of iridescent greens and purples make the grayling our most beautiful game fish.'

The body is a coruscation of light and colour, diversely described.

> 'Head and back a deep purple while the sides are a riot of purple blue and copper with tinges of pink and pale blue'.
>
> 'Purplish-blue with a golden tinge along the back'.
>
> 'Deep purple back with small dark irregular spots on the sides, the stomach a brilliant white with a fringe of gold'.
>
> 'A deep green back overlaid with purple'.

Perhaps there is no more evocative description than that I came across in *Montana Time* (1992) by John Barness. 'Some people call them freshwater sailfish because grayling wear a dorsal fin as egregious as Dolly Parton's breasts. But except for that fin, they're subtle compositions – streamlined silver was with almost subliminal purples and golds. The overall effect is not unlike 1961 Cadillac tailfins welded to a Rolls Royce … '

Another favourite description of its colouring, given to a typical North Country fish, is by an unnamed angler quoted by W. Carter Platts in *Grayling Fishing* … 'its sides were slightly "oxidised" silver mail, fading into milk white on the belly and shading off into dark olive on the back, but these colours were, as the fish was held at different angles to the light, shot with purple and pale gold; indeed seen in one light the whole of the side displayed one continuous pale golden sheen.' I have yet to find a description of the grayling that is less than flattering.

They have largish scales in parallel rows. The black spots along the flanks form markings unique to each fish. There is no evidence that certain spot patterns are common to specific rivers. Unusually many Scandinavian grayling of the same species have no spots at all. The most significant characteristic of the fish is its huge dorsal fin and it is easiest to distinguish the cock and hen fish from its shape. When the fin is pulled forward so that it is fully erect, the rear spines on the male will trail to the rear but those of the female will not. At spawning time the male's dorsal fin is usually more brightly coloured.

The shape of the grayling's eye differs quite visibly from the trout's. The pear-shaped iris is indicative of an aperture adapted to bottom feeding. Interestingly, all freshwater fish fall within two categories dependent on the retinal pigments in the eye. Some have vitamin A1 and A2 based pigments and others have only one pigment, usually A2. Studies by Professor W.R.A. Muntz and others[1] have shown that paired pigments are an adaptation for surface feeding but single A2 based retinas are specialised for bottom feeders. Trout have both pigments whereas grayling have the single A2 pigment.

The mouth of the grayling indicates that the fish is basically a bottom feeder and spends most of its time on or very near the river bed. Much of its food is taken from the bottom or from the drift in the lower third of the water, nevertheless the grayling is a free riser to surface food despite the fact that, by general concensus, its mouth is to some extent unsuited to this practice. The upper jaw slightly protrudes over the lower one, making it ideally suited to bottom feeding on the river bed. However, my friend Lars-Åke Olsson, who has considerable experience of Swedish grayling, maintains that grayling have the perfect mouth shape for surface feeding. The longer upper lip is able, within the split second of the rise, to close over the fly more easily than if the the lips were of equal length. The protruding upper lip more efficiently envelopes the surface fly. The grayling's willingness to feed on the surface, in the upper layers and close to the stream bed make them the perfect fly fisher's fish.

[1] *The Grayling Society Newsletter,* Autumn 1978 'The Feeding Relationships and Growth of Trout and Grayling' by Thomas Steven

The position of grayling close to the bottom means that they will always have the widest possible view of the surface. A grayling resting on the bottom will see surface food in its window sooner than a trout higher in the water. If the window is unrippled and a clear view is provided, grayling will see surface flies further upstream than a trout in a typical lie nearer the surface. Of course grayling have much further to move to intercept surface food. As the fish rises to the surface this circular window progressively decreases in size.

When a grayling rises to surface food it usually approaches it vertically, dropping downstream and even tilting back slightly before breaking the surface; a more precise process than for trout. In slower water, good-sized grayling sometimes follow a foot or two downstream before finally committing themselves to take the fly. Sometimes in faster water, they also may noticeably accelerate over the last third of the rise, especially if coming up from three feet or more of water – perhaps they fear the insect may fly off or that the current will take it away. On a fast, rocky river the current flow at the river bed is slower than at the surface and the rising fish speeds up to compensate for the speed of the surface food. I have observed that quite often grayling may rise more in the manner of trout, without tilting vertically to take surface food. This is also a necessity for bigger grayling in shallow water, where their body length is greater than the depth of water. If a forty centimetre grayling had to rise vertically in a depth of twenty centimetres, it would be impossible. It would be a sight to behold, with parts of the grayling being visible above the surface, with considerable surface disturbance, but this just doesn't happen. Consequently, it seems that the protruding lip does not necessitate the fish being in a vertical position; merely sometimes, perhaps where depth, current speed and the grayling size are suitable, this occurs. Lars-Åke Olsson describes the protruding upper lip as the perfect mechanism for taking a surface fly as the upper lip halts its downstream movement and closes over the fly.

In low slow water Oliver Edwards and Bernard Benson have observed many Wharfe grayling, some of them big ones, rising quite differently to the normal grayling rise. The rise is a very leisurely sip, with the grayling moving forward almost in a 'head and tail' rise more associated with trout. The neb of the grayling breaks the surface, followed by the striped red dorsal fin before quickly disappearing. Just occasionally, the dorsal fin is followed by the upper tip of the tail scything through the surface.

From about the third century[2] freshly caught grayling have had a reputation for smelling like thyme, and then in 1895 F.M. Walbran and others later suggested they had the odour of cucumber. To my sense of smell, there is no trace of cucumber. What I do know is that grayling definitely have their own unique odour, a veritable Chanel No.5 to the dedicated thymallophile.

Over many years the protagonists have argued their opinions as to whether or not the grayling is a game fish, or a coarse fish, or whether it is somewhere between the two. Over the years its scientific name has been expressed variously as *Salmo thymallus*, giving it the distinction of being a member of the salmon family, *Coregonus thymallus*, erroneously classing it with the whitefish family which spawns much earlier than the grayling, and *Thymallus vulgaris* and others. We have finally classified it as *Thymallus thymallus*, in a family of its own but within the salmon order. The difficulties of the decision ichthyologists have faced concerns the complexity of the grayling's physiology and lifecycle when compared with the salmonid's and other freshwater fish. Various aspects of its natural history can be classified in more than one group. From an angler's point of view, we reduce the classification of freshwater fish into two categories; they fall under either the game or coarse fish headings. Depending upon one's viewpoint, the grayling is pushed under one of these two classifications. Grayling much prefer to live alongside salmonids and they will happily co-exist in the same stream whereas in many coarse fisheries they would not survive.

As a game fish, the grayling has in its favour the tell-tale badge of true upper-class breeding, the adipose fin, the hallmark of the salmon family (but which is also shared with the whitefish family). Its bone formation, lacking in the gristle-based dorsal bones resulting in more flesh on the bone inclines it towards the salmon family. The third aspect is that it inhabits the same stretches of rivers as does the brown trout. Fourthly, and probably most importantly from the game fisher's viewpoint, is its willingness to take wet fly and nymph and to rise freely to the dry fly. Its readiness to co-operate with the fly fisherman is the single strongest

[2] Claudius Aelian translated by the Rev W. Houghton in *British Freshwater Fishes*, 1884. 'When captured it has a remarkable odour – not that other kinds are destitute of a fishy smell – so that you would say you had in your hands a freshy gathered piece of thyme.'

argument for classifying it as a game fish. There are few today who would not class it as such. Most of the objectors are chalk stream fly fishers who having paid tidy sums to fish for large trout, are naturally infuriated that their sport is subject to interruption by small summer grayling. Spring grayling, and perhaps on the chalk streams, early summer grayling, put up little resistance on being hooked, and if I had patiently stalked a four pound trout and an eight ounce grayling had rushed to snatch my fly then the grayling might be cursed. But catching out-of-season, out-of-condition fish, on inappropriate tackle, is no basis on which to judge grayling. It should not detract from the truth that in its season the grayling fights as well as a trout of equal weight.

HABITAT

Grayling are very selective in their choice of habitat and attempts at introducing them into previously unstocked waters can be easily thwarted unless the particular standards are met. Limestone and chalk based streams are preferred where there is unpolluted, well-oxygenated water with a good food supply. Acidic waters are not tolerated but neutral waters such as the Tay and Tweed hold good stocks of grayling. At the slightest hint of pollution grayling will disappear well before trout. Grayling require less oxygen than trout but more than coarse species. The result is that the upper reaches of a river may contain trout only; further downstream, a combination of trout and grayling, and below that, grayling and a few coarse fish, and in the slower deeper stretches, coarse fish only. Few rivers fit this description exactly but the pattern is visible. Other reasons for distribution within a river are water temperature and clarity and the nature of the riverbed – ideally a combination of gravel, small stones and sand. Rarely are grayling found over a solid rock riverbed. They are very sensitive to changes in temperature and will move in search of cooler or warmer water. The coldest weather will drive them into the deep pools, and at warm summer temperatures they will be found in the faster streamy glides, in pocket water or even at the very heads of riffles. Research has convinced me that they are not as nomadic as I once thought but that they will adopt different lies determined by water temperature throughout the season. It is the streamy glides that are most associated with grayling and where most will live from June to

November. A leisurely flow of a moderate pace and constant depth is preferred but the cold of winter will drive them into the deeper warmer water. Over the course of twelve months grayling feeding intensity varies and it broadly follows the change in water temperature.

Sometimes grayling will be found in quite rough water, where one might think there was hardly a lie that offered any ease at all. I have caught many summer grayling from the heads of riffles which I had ignored for years as grayling lies. Two methods I have adopted have produced many grayling from water that I would have passed over fifteen years ago. They are the use of heavy bugs and caddis larvae imitations fished on the bottom, and the now famous Klinkhamer Special, which can be fished in the roughest of water and attracts grayling across a few feet of turbulent current. Both have radically altered fishing in fast water. In recent seasons my biggest grayling from freestone rivers have all been caught at the heads of pools or high up a riffle. There they have been able to find a comfortable lie in the calmer water close to the stream bed or behind a stone. Whereas trout will often move out of their resting lies to the main food lane during nymph activity or a hatch of fly, grayling usually feed in the lies they adopt. During a hatch, trout will move into the head of a pool to feed and may oust the smaller grayling from the prime positions. However, I haven't found that bigger grayling are intimidated by trout in this way; rather they have stayed in the better feeding positions and not given in to trout pressure. The smaller grayling drop down a pool if trout move up but I've often caught big grayling from the prime positions alongside good trout who have moved into the area to feed.

I have occasionally observed grayling actively searching the river bed for food, and often they have been bigger than average fish. They have picked up and moved pebbles and gravel in their mouths, foraging for shrimps, nymphs and caddis larvae beneath the stones. Their mouths could not be more suitably shaped for the process.

On very few occasions have I seen grayling on the fin just inches below the surface. Usually they prefer to stay deep and rise rapidly from the bottom to pick off surface food. But I recall one June or July evening whilst fishing a stream containing both trout and grayling that I found myself casting to three shadowy figures lying just below the surface in about four feet of water that were, every thirty seconds or so, picking off passing duns. So near were they to the surface that I presumed them to be trout and watched them for a minute or two. It became obvious that two of the three fish were grayling and that one of the grayling wasn't rising at all but taking the emerging nymph in or just below the surface film. I caught one of the three, a grayling of about a pound – a good fish for the stream – and the remaining two bolted for cover. As a rule, it is a very rare thing in my experience to find grayling stationed so near the surface except occasionally on the chalk streams where grayling may lie closer to the surface above a weed bed. Of European grayling, Charles Ritz wrote[3] that during evening rises, for instance, a sedge hatch on the River Traun, grayling would adopt trout behaviour and remain just below the surface for feeding on top. This is very rare in Britain. A grayling that rises to a fly on the surface and decides not to take it at the last moment or misses it, will not remain at the surface waiting for the next fly but return to its original lie before rising again.

If the average size grayling for a particular river are to be found in the streamy water, then the big fish, those that have escaped capture the longest will often be found elsewhere. True, there have been times when I have caught much larger than average fish from amongst a shoal but invariably my bigger fish have come from places that I suspected of holding only a few grayling. Very deep holes, deep backwaters at the edge of faster currents, under a steep bank edge, under a well protected low bridge, the heads of riffles, all have been places that have regularly yielded bigger than average fish. I presume this is so because the lies have offered protection from predators and were difficult for the angler to fish. Experience reveals that on rainfed rivers the bigger fish in a shoal tend to be at the head, first in the feeding order. On clear chalk streams, where I've been able to study the composition of autumn shoals, this order does not necessarily prevail. The bigger fish can be expected at any position and invariably are constantly on the move within the shoal. Perhaps the food supply is so great that there is no need to compete.

For the most part grayling are a shoal fish, especially on the chalk streams. But mature fish on rainfed rivers are often more widely scattered. They adopt home territories in much smaller groups of half or dozen or less, or even singly. Only in December to February do they move to the deeper pools to form part of the larger shoals. Research[4] on the River Dee

[3] *A Fly Fisher's Life*, 1959

[4] *Journal of the Grayling Society*, Autumn 1986 'Grayling in the Welsh Dee, Part 2 Movements'

by Dr John Woolland has shown that a high percentage of captured grayling which were moved about 250 metres from their capture sites, returned to their original lies. The majority returned again after removal. The implication is that grayling adopt home territories, and even after being caught will return to the same lie.

In the summer grayling are found in runs and pools but prefer the steady glides of a constant depth to the deep pools. At any time of year depressions and hollows of just a few inches into the stream bed will offer attractive lies out of the main current but close to food. In higher temperatures they will also be found in very fast water. Another good summer and autumn lie is at the tail of a pool, towards the run-off into the next riffle. Here the water shallows and grayling do not have far to move to intercept surface food. All fish adopt lies that best suit their feeding (grayling close to the river bed) and allow them to remain comfortable in terms of water flow and temperature. In slightly high water grayling may be found nearer the sides in calmer water or further downstream from their usual lies, eg, nearer the tail of a pool where the flow is slower. In very high and turbid water I have found grayling right under the bank in quite shallow water, or in the eddies behind islands.

Although less territorial than trout, when grouped in small numbers or singly, they become more territorial, especially so at spawning time. Around December they begin to shoal up in water of one to two metres in depth prior to spawning, and places that held grayling in late summer or October can be empty of them two or three months later. This shoaling habit can be both infuriating and rewarding for the angler. The main problem is finding a shoal. The difficult problem of locating them on a strange river is solved only by fishing out the likely pools. In clear chalk streams against a background of gravel, keen eyesight and polarised sunglasses may be sufficient but on most rainfed rivers a visible sighting is impossible. Once a shoal is located very often what follows is a very entertaining period of fishing. On clear chalk streams in October I've seen shoals of sixty or more fish; one can only guess at their number in the deep pools in February. Whether on fly or bait, it is possible to take many fish on successive casts. Just a year or two ago, when dry-fly fishing in October I managed to land and release more than forty grayling in exactly one hour's fishing. Improbable but true. I hardly moved three paces and my fly could not have been covering more than twenty square yards of the surface. I probably missed a third of the rises and would guess from previous experience that I interested fewer than half the fish in the shoal.

For a wild fish, grayling can be very tolerant of man, especially one in waders slowly edging closer. Rarely will wild trout allow such familiarity, although domesticated hatchery fish may. I have watched the behaviour of ex-hatchery trout in some of our most revered rivers and have been extremely disappointed how such fish are so plainly stupid and easily caught. Many stocked trout tolerate the presence of man long after grayling have departed. But having gone, grayling will return, and you may not have long to wait. Even if a shoal moves away or partially scatters, it soon reforms and begins to feed again. Similarly, when grayling are alerted to a bug or nymph continually moving through the shoal they may cease to feed. Offer another pattern, or rest them for five minutes, and they will reveal just how short their memories are.

DISTRIBUTION

A number of attempts have been made to explain the originally erratic distribution of grayling in the United Kingdom. One of the most prolific grayling-holding river systems is that of the Yorkshire Ouse. The Ouse itself probably holds no grayling but they abound in most of its tributaries. More than a dozen rivers and streams in North Yorkshire hold good stocks of indigenous grayling. Other areas holding natural stocks include the Derbyshire rivers, Wye, Dove and Derwent, the Welsh Dee, Severn and Wye, the Lancashire Ribble and the Hampshire Avon and their tributary streams. The indigenous stock of English and Welsh grayling was thinly spread with concentrated pockets. There were none at all in Scotland and there still are none in Ireland.

Today's wider distribution is solely the result of artificial stocking, which began in the latter half of the nineteenth century. The Test was the most important water to receive stocks from other rivers. In 1816 the first batch of grayling was introduced and thrived. Some years later the Itchen was also stocked. In 1855, the Scots (perhaps bored with catching salmon) realised the sporting qualities of grayling and released three dozen mature Derbyshire fish into the Clyde. Two years later 18,000 impregnated ova were released and 2000 in the Nith. Today the Tweed is one of the best grayling rivers in Scotland, but their presence there is due entirely to an accidental introduction into its tributary, the Teviot. In 1860, the banks of an artificially stocked pond at Monteviot overflowed and grayling were freed into the river system. The Tay was the next, in 1880, and in the same year the Cumbrian Eden received an illegal introduction of fry.

The West Country streams were also stocked around this time. Frank Buckland's book, *Fish Hatching* (1863) mentions the River Thames being stocked with 2000 grayling around 1860, although this does not necessarily imply that these were the first non-indigenous stocks. Through the years more rivers have been stocked and today more and more clubs want grayling to supplement their fishing.

British grayling need running water for spawning. They are naturally present in two British stillwaters, Llyn Tegid (Lake Bala) in North Wales and Gouthwaite Reservoir in North Yorkshire. Llyn Tegid is a natural lake from which the River Dee flows. Gouthwaite was created by damming the River Nidd. In both waters grayling have access to spawning streams. There are least two smaller artificial lakes into which grayling have been introduced, but I have not heard of reports of them breeding. In 1975, 8,000 grayling fry were stocked in a fishless hill loch in north Perthshire[5]. No evidence of breeding exists but survivors of the original introduction were present in 1991. In Canada there are very many lakes containing grayling but these too are dependent upon rivers for grayling to spawn. In cold Scandinavian lakes grayling are known to spawn along the lake margins.

In Appendix A, I have attempted to compile a complete record of every grayling river and stream in the U.K. (two hundred or so). Some of the rivers may hold only a few of the species and would not warrant attention specifically for grayling. Some mentioned have grayling only in their middle or upper reaches but others are very prolific waters. My original smaller list was compiled with the help of David Liversedge, Vice President of the Grayling Society, and with the assistance of some of the old Water Authorities.

[5] *Scottish Grayling History and Biology of the Populations*, Ross Gardiner, SOFAD

LIFECYCLE

If only grayling could achieve the phenomenal growth rates of some hatchery-reared rainbow trout. I would love to encounter a four or five pound grayling in a rough northern river. With its huge dorsal fin erect, holding itself in a strong downstream current, it would be a match for the most skilful and patient of anglers. Sadly such fish appear only in the dreams of the most dedicated grayling fishers, for there are very few rivers in the country that may hold a four pound specimen. I have caught grayling of over two and a half pounds in the fast waters of the River Kaitum in Swedish Lapland and lost bigger fish in the fight. These big grayling in fast water are a tremendous challenge on appropriate tackle. The erect dorsal fin almost doubles the fish's body size and in a current too turbulent to wade, unforgettable battles ensue. Big grayling often fight to the very last and put up a very spirited resistance. Although they don't often jump, northern European grayling will do so, sometimes two or three times in fast water. I can assure you that leaping two pound plus grayling in a big fast river are unforgettable. No wonder that my friend Lars-Åke Olsson refers to Swedish Lapland as the 'Land of the Jumping Grayling'. My experience is that bigger grayling which fight until exhausted need and deserve to be treated with care and patiently nursed before they are released.

The current U.K. record grayling stands at four pounds three ounces with a fish from the River Frome in Dorset. I regard the three pound figure as the equivalent of a four minute mile, an exclusive club which is constantly eluding me. When Antony Witherby, my first publisher and once in a blue moon grayling angler, read this comment he coyly revealed in his most modest manner that he had once caught a grayling in excess of three pounds and "there wasn't much to it, actually." Thus the publisher asserted his angling superiority over a mere author. Certainly there have been well documented grayling of over four pounds a century ago. In 1891 two fishermen on the River Test caught three grayling for a total weight of twelve pounds and lost one fish estimated at five pounds. Sadly those ample days for the Test and other streams are probably long gone. The fish that once held the record was one of seven pounds and two ounces caught in the River Meglum in 1949. I have seen the very poor photograph that exists, and close scrutiny reveals that far from being a grayling the fish was probably a salmon or seatrout kelt. In

1968 this 'grayling' was deleted from the record books. But before huge grayling like this one are dismissed out of hand, far bigger have been caught in Scandinavia; the biggest that I am aware of is one of fourteen and a half pounds (6.7 kg) from Finland.[6]

The main reason why there are so few big grayling is that they are short lived, usually no longer than five or six years. However, they may live to twice this age and over twenty years in Scandinavia. Growth rates in most habitats flatten out after three or four years but not at the extreme northern limits of grayling territory. In northern Scandinavia and Russia, after slow early growth, they continue to grow steadily to much greater weights. In British rivers the main seasonal growth period is between April and November with relatively little growth during winter.

I used to believe that in the UK it was rivers like the Test – where there were good conditions for record grayling – that would one day produce a really big grayling of four to five pounds. But now I think that the pressures on some chalk streams from the sheer numbers of hatchery trout is so great that the prospects for producing a potential record grayling are slim. My opinion is that the likely rivers are currently the Frome, Welsh Wye and the Tweed or Tay. The last three have a larger area of river bed so that statistically the odds improve; secondly, for much of their course, they are not fished for grayling because it interferes with salmon fishing and thirdly, they provide a diet supplemented by high protein salmon eggs at a time when food is in shorter supply. The Welsh Dee is a possible candidate, but as it is fished for grayling already it may not be so likely as the Tweed or Tay. Incidentally, there is no evidence that grayling disturb salmon redds and hunt for eggs, but they will take them from the drift. Scottish anglers have told me of seeing small shoals of grayling downstream of spawning salmon and sea trout. They stay well below, out of attacking distance, but close enough to take the eggs that have missed the redds and are caught by the current.

Grayling share a spawning season with coarse fish so do not compete with trout for spawning grounds. Very occasionally grayling in the same river spawn as early as April or as late as July, but not during the

[6] Elorants, A. (1985). *Grayling Thymallus thymallus in the lower part of the Rautalampi watercourse, Finnish Lake District.* Verh, Internat. Verein. Limnol. 22, 2555–2559. This reference is in English. Earlier references are in Finnish. They relate to a fish caught in 1956 in Lake Konnevesesi

same year. During the period leading up to late-April and May when the fish usually spawns, the female is noticeably fatter than the male, and the male much darker in colour. At spawning time, the shoals break up and the mature fish congregate over light gravel. The males jealously guard the spawning beds from trout and rival grayling. Roy Shaw, who has closely observed grayling spawning in the chalk waters of the Driffield Canal, has noticed as many as a dozen males to every female, but observations elsewhere suggest that this is unusual. After a period of frantic rushing about by both males and females, pairs will close, with the cock fish invariably to the right of the hen, and with the cock's huge dorsal fin held over the hen's body. The male's tail puts pressure on the wrist of the female's tail ensuring that close lateral and downward contact is maintained. Both bodies vibrate and quiver together so the gravel is pushed away by their tail movements. At the climax of this frenzy, the females lay their eggs, and seconds afterwards the male releases his milt on them. Grayling lay more eggs than brown trout. The figure varies in proportion to the weight of the females, anywhere between 7,000 and 37,500 per kilo of body weight[7]; between 3,000–6,000 is usual for smaller fish.

At the time of spawning, male grayling can be extremely aggressive in defending the area of the gravel bed on which they will release their milt. They will fight off intruding trout intent on eating the female's eggs. Trout anglers frequently claim that grayling thrive in a fishery that contains both species, and that trout stocks suffer because of the prolific egg production of grayling when compared with trout. Trout ensure that the level of grayling stocks is restricted by spawn consumption and predation of young grayling.

The eggs are about 3 mm in diameter, and after a period of about two to four weeks, depending on water temperature (a steady 10°C will take 18 days, or approximately 180 degree days in the U.K.), they will emerge from the gravel as alevins approximately 12–18 mm long. These young larvae shoal close to the surface and the river bank until they reach about 25 mm, when they return to deeper, faster, water. They grow faster than trout or salmon at this age and will reach 100–180 mm by winter. Growth is fairly rapid, especially in the chalk streams, until maturity at

[7] Blachuta, J., Kowalewski, M. & Witkowski, A. 1982 Fecundity of three grayling (*Thymallus thymallus* (L.)) populations of various growth rate. Zoologica Poloniae 29

two or three years of age for males, and three or four years for females. Fish will then be between 20 and 40 cm depending upon growth rates.

The average size of fish varies from river to river. In most of the rainfed rivers of the North of England, an average fish may be 22–25 cm. But in a chalk stream the average length might be 5 cm longer and the fish fatter. The appendix on page 147 gives an insight into different growth rates on British rivers. Ross Gardiner[8] offered the hypothesis that in Scottish grayling where the fastest growths were achieved in the larger rivers, 'that this may be, at least in part, a density related effect, as a result of a shortage of suitable spawning or nursery areas in large rivers limiting the numbers of grayling or competitor species.' Dr John Woolland[9] also suggests that the differences in growth rates between the upper Dee (slower growth) and the Dee at Corwen (faster growth) may have been due to the different grayling population densities. The greater densities were found at the upper site.

In river fisheries brown trout are stocked at least once a year, possibly more often. Grayling are very rarely stocked once a population has established itself. Most fisheries stock with trout of takeable size, anything from 25 to 45 cm or even larger. All these trout are carnivorous and will feed upon grayling eggs and fry. In a stocked river it is possible that trout will oust grayling from their lies and prey on their young. Sometimes the presence of grayling in a river has been an easy scapegoat for trout anglers looking to blame something for poor fishing. I contend this is rarely the truth and that the reasons are likely to lie elsewhere. It is much more likely that overstocking with trout has led to a reduction in grayling stocks.

[8] *Scottish Grayling: History and Biology of the Populations* , SOFAD, Ross Gardiner

[9] *Journal of the Grayling Society* Autumn 1987 'Grayling in the Welsh Dee: Age and Growth'

3

FOOD

'For baits for great fish, keep this rule especially: When you have taken a great fish, open up the belly, and whatever you find in it, make that your bait, for it is best.'

Aelian, circa 200 AD

BOTH TROUT AND GRAYLING feed upon those items most readily available to them in their local habitat. Because they live so closely together it is inevitable that there will be considerable overlap in their diets and there may be competition for the available food. This is reflected in growth rate studies where the two co-exist. However, there is more competition within the same species population for the available food. Inter-species competition only becomes a factor in relative growth or survival rates when food is in short supply. If food is plentiful, consumption by one species has a minimal effect on the other.

It is easy for anglers to form opinions and invent theories on many aspects of fishing based solely on their own limited observations. Sometimes they get it right but more often supposition, conjecture and wishful thinking hide the truth. I am as guilty as anyone. Only the fishery scientists can settle some issues. Fortunately there has been research into aspects of grayling behaviour that is of interest to the angler and my hope is this will continue. The Grayling Society, the Grayling Research Trust, the Environment Agency, and the universities will continue to be important in this respect. One fisheries scientist whose researches I have drawn on over the years is Dr John Woolland. His studies often have a direct interest for the angler and again I am very grateful for permission to quote from his findings[1].

Knowing the feeding habits of grayling, including seasonal, daily, or hourly variations, is very important for fly fishers. While rising fish reveal much to the observant angler, it is with those unseen subsurface feeders that we could use more help.

Over a five year period, Dr Woolland conducted a survey into the stomach contents of 411 grayling on the Welsh Dee to determine their feeding habits. Simultaneously, he did the same for fish in Llyn Tegid, but as stillwater grayling are of minor interest to most anglers I have omitted these findings. Grayling of other rivers will never mimic those of the Dee but the data offers an excellent guide to the feeding trends of grayling in other rainfed rivers.

Seasonal Variation in Feeding Intensity

Studies on grayling have generally shown that the feeding intensity is high and that grayling with empty stomachs are rare. The seasonal feeding intensity of grayling in the River Dee is shown in figure 1. The mean stomach fullness never fell below one third full and was rarely less than half full. No empty stomachs were found in River Dee grayling.

Feeding intensity was closely related to water temperature. Periods of low feeding activity coincided with minimum and maximum temperatures, and periods of high feeding activity coincided with intermediate temperatures. Feeding was at its lowest in February and March when water temperatures were also at their lowest. The peak feeding activity was in the late spring and early summer, but was generally high throughout most of the year.

[1]*Journal of the Grayling Society*, Spring 1987 'Grayling in the Welsh Dee, Part 3 Feeding' *Journal of the Grayling Society*, Spring 1988 'The Feeding Relationships of grayling and trout in the Welsh Dee'

Composition of the Diet

The composition of the diet of River Dee grayling by % number, volume and occurrence is shown in table 1. Grayling were found to consume both a large variety and a large number of food organisms, with a mean number of 101 food items per stomach.

Trichopteran (caddis) larvae were by far the most important food item. The main species eaten were *Potamophylax latipennis*[2], *Glossoma conformis*, *Goera pilosa*, *Hydropsyche instabilis*[3] and *Agapetus fuscipes*[4]. Trichopteran larvae were eaten in large quantities throughout the year, with a peak during the winter and early spring. Older grayling ate more of these larvae than young grayling. Small larvae such as *Agapetus fuscipes* were preferred by young fish and larger species such as *Potamophylax latipennis* were eaten by older grayling.

Aerial insects were the next major food category, with those of terrestrial origin being more important than those of aquatic origin. The terrestrial insects eaten were from the orders Diptera (mainly Empididae and Bibionidae[5], Hymenoptera (Ichneumonidae, Apidae[6], Formica[7] and Vespa[8], and Hemiptera (mostly Aphidae[9]. The most commonly eaten aquatic aerial insects were *Ephemerella ignita*[10], *Baetis rhodani*[11] and *Leuctra fusca*[12]. Consumption of terrestrial insects was highest in heavily wooded stretches of the river. As would be expected, marked seasonal variations occurred in feeding on aerial insects, with the peak occurring from May to October, but significant numbers being taken in November, December and April. Aquatic aerial insects were eaten according to their respective emergence period with, for example, *Baetis rhodani* and *Leuctra spp* eaten in

[2] Large cinnamon sedge
[3] Grey flag
[4] Micro grey sedge
[5] Black gnats
[6] Bees
[7] Ants
[8] Wasps
[9] Aphids
[10] Blue-winged olive
[11] Large dark olive
[12] Needle fly

the spring and autumn, and *Chloroperla torrentium*[13] and *Isoperla grammatica*[14] eaten during the summer. Aerial insects became increasingly less important in the diet of older grayling with a progressive tendency towards bottom feeding.

Ephemeropteran nymphs (*Ephemerella ignita, Baetis rhodani* and *Heptagenia sulphurea*[15]), Plecopteran nymphs (*Isoperla grammatica, Chloroperla torrentium,* and *Leuctra spp.*) and dipteran larvae (*Chironomidae*) were next in dietary importance. Peaks of consumption of ephemeropteran and plecopteran nymphs occurred just before and during their emergence periods when these nymphs were most accessible to feeding grayling. Ephemeropteran nymphs were eaten in greatest quantities in June and July. Plecopteran nymphs and dipteran larvae were eaten to the greatest extent in the spring. They were also common throughout the winter but less so in the summer. Chironomidae larvae were a major food item during the winter.

Other items found in grayling stomachs included Crustacea (*Gammarus pulex*[16] and *Asellus meridianus*), mollusca (*Ancylastrum fluviatile*[17]), Coleoptera[18], Megaloptera (*Sialis fuliginosa*[19]), Hirudinea (*Erpobdella octoculata*) and Corixidae. Four grayling were found to contain fish in their stomachs, these were two bullheads, one stickleback and one minnow. Only nine fish eggs (grayling) were found in the stomachs examined.

Summary

1 Grayling in the Welsh Dee fed actively throughout the year, although some reduction in feeding occurred at both very low and high water temperatures.
2 The main food items of River Dee grayling were trichopteran (caddis) larvae and aerial insects.

[13] Small yellow Sally, now renamed as *Siphonoperla torrentium*
[14] Yellow Sally
[15] Yellow May dun
[16] shrimp
[17] snail
[18] beetles
[19] alder

3 Plecopteran (stonefly) nymphs, dipteran larvae and Crustacea were mostly eaten in the winter and spring, while aerial insects and ephemeropteran nymphs were eaten during the summer and early autumn. Dee grayling ate large quantities of trichopteran larvae throughout the year.

4 Grayling in the River Dee were found to be predominantly bottom feeders, but with considerable quantities of mid-water and surface food being added to the diet when this was available. Food organisms were taken from exposed positions on the river bed, and were also rooted out from among stones and bottom deposits. Grayling generally fed on organisms which were most numerous or most accessible.'

In comparison studies[20] of grayling and brown trout in the River Dee, Dr Woolland's findings are also very interesting. He observes that 'Difference in diets also occurred with age, most particularly in relation to the consumption of surface food which increased in age with trout, but decreased with age in grayling.' Unsurprisingly, trout and grayling habitats and their feeding locations influenced their diet. 'Grayling generally laid close to the river bed and ate fewer aerial insects than trout which fed from a mid-water position. Grayling also tended to occupy midstream positions in water of medium depth in runs at the tail of pools and ate caddis larvae typical of these locations such as *Agapetus* and *Glossoma spp.* Trout, on the other hand, were located along the river edges close to undercut banks and overhanging trees.' My own fishing experience confirms this last observation. For twenty-five years I have fished a small North Yorkshire stream, a tributary of the Rye, containing both wild trout and grayling. My advice to visiting fly fishers has always been to fish the margins for trout and the centre of the river for grayling. I'm pleased the 'official' findings confirm a mere angler's theory.

Surveys of chalk stream grayling show that shrimps are the principal food source throughout the year. They are the most abundant food and are readily available from the stream bed, the main feeding area. My own examination of stomach contents revealed that shrimp are often the only food consumed and invariably in excess of 75% of the total by weight or

[20] *The Journal of the Grayling Society*, Spring 1988

number. A good hatch of duns will always attract interest, as will pre-emergence nymph activity, but for 90% of the time shrimps will be the major food source. A chalk stream angler might be tempted to look no further than a shrimp imitation for all his grayling fishing. In autumn many do and fare no worse, often better, than those of us with a dozen different artificials.

I am unaware of any surveys conducted into the variation in grayling feeding intensity throughout the day. More often than not they will feed when food is readily available. Just occasionally they will ignore obvious food until some imaginary dinner gong has sounded. I recall one late October day on the Driffield Beck when I had struggled to catch four or five fish for as many hours effort. The shoals had ignored my nymphs and bugs, until suddenly, at about three-thirty, the shoal I was casting to, which I had fruitlessly covered comprehensively twice before that day, began to feed. My final forty five minutes produced twenty grayling on one bug pattern. I am sure that shrimps and nymphs were available to them all day but they hadn't been in the feeding mood. It pays to persevere with grayling because they feed at some time on most days.

GRAYLING AND THE CADDIS

Examine almost any area of river bed, any sizeable stone or patch of weed and there caddis larvae will be found. No part of the river bed escapes their presence; each type of substratum is attractive to many of the approximately 200 British caddis species and they abound in great quantities wherever grayling are found. Dr Woolland's survey of Dee grayling diets confirmed caddis larvae in the stomachs in 92.5% of those examined; the highest incidence of any food source. There is a very high probability that in rainfed rivers like the Dee, on any one day nine out of ten grayling will feed on the larvae at some stage. In the same survey, the larvae made up 20% by number and 49.7% by volume of the total diet. Conversely, evidence of chalk stream grayling[21] diets suggest a consumption of less than 10% by number. No doubt the ready supply of shrimps and snails accounts for the difference.

[21] Survey published in Trout and Grayling, An Angler's Natural History (A & C Black), 1979, by Norman Maclean

In the original edition of *The Grayling Angler* I wrote that the river fly fisherman would find the slow moving larvae impossible to imitate with an artificial, and that the only time the caddis could be copied was at the pupal and adult stage. How wrong could I be! Since that fateful statement I have been corrected scores of times by obliging grayling. Twenty years ago, few, if any, British fly fishers were using caddis larvae imitations on rivers and I was not aware of any British representation of the free swimming caddis larvae. It was only during the 1980s that we looked at North American and Scandinavian larvae imitations and adopted them here. What a difference they have made to both grayling and trout fishing.

The eggs of the caddis hatch into grub-like larvae. Most species build a case or tube of small stones, sand, twigs or other vegetable matter or material from the stream bed, bound together by a silken thread. Many species build distinctive cases and the case shape and construction is a major clue to species identification. The larva moves by sticking its head, thorax and legs out of the end of the case and dragging it along. There are a few free-swimming species which do not build cases. These non case-makers represent a quarter (by number) of the caddis larvae in the Woolland diet survey. The percentage of free-swimming caddis in the Dee and other rivers is likely to be less than 5% of the total caddis larvae population, and yet they figure relatively highly in the diet. There must be a good reason for this. My anthropomorphic response is that the free swimming species either taste better or are more palatable to digest than larvae covered in grit or perhaps it is that they appear more frequently in the drift. Thus, imitating them is extremely important on many grayling rivers. Grayling have often been observed mouthing stones and rejecting them or moving stones on the riverbed. Perhaps they are actively searching for food like the free swimming larvae rather than waiting for the current to bring them along

The cased larva is fairly static on the river bed, clinging to stones, gravel and weed. When it does move, it is at a very slow pace. It is quite possible to represent these with artificials fished bouncing along the bottom. Perhaps the most attractive of recently devised patterns are those with an imitation of the wriggling larva extended well out of its case; Oliver Edwards's Peeking Caddis, inspired by the Leadhead Nymph of Hans van Klinken, being an excellent example. The non case-makers live between stones, spinning a net for their domicile, but are neither protected nor weighed down by a case. These, and more frequently, the free swimmers are likely to be dislodged by the current. Once adrift they are very vulnerable to predation. I have found an imitation of the free swimming *Rhyacophila* or *Hydropsyche* species is very effective when fished in a riffle.

Some caddis larvae are vegetarian, but as anyone who has kept an aquatic insect aquarium will tell you, many species are carnivorous. They eat all types of aquatic insects including ephemeropteran nymphs, so important to good dun hatches and dry fly fishing. Richard Walker pointed out to me in 1981 that in some parts of the River Test where there are no grayling, caddis larvae abound and have a noticeable effect on the quality of dry-fly fishing. In those stretches that also hold grayling there are fewer caddis and the ephemerid life is far more active.

Whether free swimming or case building, all larvae have common characteristics. They have three major body sections: head, thorax and abdomen. The head and thorax are usually much darker coloured than the abdomen. There are three pairs of legs, one pair to each thoracic segment. The abdomen has ten segments, each with gills in the form of filaments on the underside or hairs all over.

After about eleven months the larva seals its case which is anchored to a rock or weed. Inside the case the larva pupates and within a silken cocoon the wings, legs and adult organs form. Eventually the emerging or pharate, adult chews its way through the case wall and aided by natural buoyancy, swims strongly to the surface. The pharate adult, wrongly but commonly called a pupa, is broadly similar to the adult in colour and size. The emergence from pharate adult/pupa to winged adult usually takes place at the surface and the emerging adult is free to fly away, leaving the pupal shuck behind.

The key characteristics of the pupa are a head, and three thoracic segments and nine abdominal segments. The immature wings extend up to half the body length on the lower side of the thorax. The abdomen is usually a lighter colour than the thorax but on some species there are dark markings on the dorsal side of the abdomen. There are six long legs under the body, of which the middle pair may be more prominent for swimming, and two long antennae sweeping over the back of the pupa.

The loose sheath surrounding the ascending pupa is transparent. In some species it would appear that a layer of gas is produced by the insect, either to aid ascent or in splitting the skin at the surface. Once at the surface the split begins at the head and down the back so that the winged adult may emerge quickly. Although previously widely accepted, recently some entomologists have disputed the existence of a gas build up within the pupal sheath. Certainly there is some translucent material surrounding the natural but this could be water within the sheath.

The migration of pupae from river bed to surface invariably attracts the attention of trout and grayling midwater and at the surface. If there is an emergence in progress, grayling may concentrate on the pupae and emerging adults to the exclusion of all other food. My experience on a wide range of rivers in the UK and elsewhere confirms this. They may rise to the adult imitation too but the pupa or emerger pattern (damp in the film or just below the surface) is far more effective. Except imediately after a caddis hatch pupae rarely turn up in surveys of grayling stomach contents. The reason is that the pupae are available for a short period. (In Scandinavia, where the caddis hatches can be both prolific and protracted, the pupae feature more often.) From exiting the pupal cocoon to flight, the process may take as little as half a minute. Conversely, larvae are available all day, every day of the year. My examination of stomach contents of grayling caught during a sedge hatch has always revealed a marked preference for the pupa, only infrequently have I found an adult sedge.

The adults of most species do not delay long on the surface and take flight almost immediately. The exceptions are exposed to predation. The adults are easily recognisable by their four roof-shaped wings covered in tiny hairs and two prominent antennae. Wings vary in size from just a few millimetres to 25 millimetres or more.

I suspect that natural adult caddis attract only a passing interest from British grayling. There are times when the newly emerged adult lingers on the surface and is consumed, and no doubt the returning egg-laying females are taken, especially in North America and Scandinavia, but pupae are far more attractive. However, the adult caddis imitation works very well in a riffle or other fast water where fish must decide quickly about passing food. Over the years I've caught many grayling on adult sedges, – there are few better general patterns than Skues' Little Red Sedge, – but usually not during a sedge hatch. In the absence of a hatch, I use the adult imitation as a search fly when wishing to fish dry. Caddis can be expected even into November so the imitation is not inappropriate.

Although sedges emerge throughout the day, the most prolific times are during warm, windless, summer evenings, continuing through dusk into darkness. Perhaps no period is more dramatic or rewarding as at the end of a hot summer day when aquatic fly hatches have been minimal and grayling lethargic. During the evening the sedges come on and they invariably attract attention. On a good day this will continue well into darkness. As the light fails, within a short time it appears as though every fish in the river is chasing ascending pupae to the surface. Splashy rises betray the pupa and emerging adults being taken from the surface film. Elsewhere in Europe, where summer grayling fishing is the norm, many more caddis pupae imitations have been devised. In Britain, where the start of our grayling season has been delayed until October, we have lost out on these marvellous opportunities for earlier grayling.

SHRIMPS

The crustacean we take to be a shrimp isn't really one at all, rather it is more closely related to the sandhoppers found at the seashore. But its appearance and general behaviour suggest to us that it is a shrimp and it has long been known by this name. The freshwater shrimp prefers to inhabit chalk and limestone-based streams, the more alkaline the water, the more it thrives. This also happens to be preferred grayling habitat. The exceptions to this preference are the waters of Northern Europe and Canada. Just as there are very few, if any, shrimps in the more acidic moorland rivers, there are no grayling either.

In the alkaline waters of a chalk stream, thousands of shrimp may inhabit a single small patch of weed; so they are an easy food source. I have often spooned chalk stream trout and grayling and found shrimp to be over 90% of the stomach contents. In the autumn and winter when nymphs are scarce and immature, when fewer sedges are active and surface food is infrequent, shrimp are the predominant food source. My small North Yorkshire stream has little weed and so relatively few shrimp. Those that I find are usually on the underside of stones or in moss. Despite the natural's comparative scarcity, even there the artificial shrimp does very well fished deep and is one of the most successful grayling patterns throughout the year.

The colour of the natural shrimp varies from a translucent grey, light olive to pale tan. Sometimes it is possible to find a fair proportion of the shrimp population with a distinctive orange spot in the centre of their bodies. The spot is a worm-like parasite that causes the shrimp to be less sensitive to light, so that it spends more time in open water instead of in weed or under stones, and is more exposed to predation. The parasite is an important source of carotenoids which are used by male sticklebacks, among other species, to develop their bright orangey-red breeding colours. It has been proven[22] that male sticklebacks actively select the infected shrimps, and I suggest that perhaps the spot is also a trigger to grayling. At spawning time the large reddish dorsal fin of the grayling is more brightly coloured than during the rest of the year. Does the bright fin colouring enhance its chances of attracting a female? If so, do grayling search out the infected shrimps for a purpose? If sticklebacks do, then perhaps grayling do too. If we ever get an answer to these questions, it might suggest a reason why grayling flies with a touch of red, orange or yellow have proved so successful, especially in the autumn and winter period prior to spawning.

The shrimp's body is usually between 12 and 18 mm. They swim in a stop-start darting motion by elongation of the segmented body which is curved at rest. They can swim very fast. Suitable imitations are easy to tie, none more so than the Killer Bug. Many are tied on curved hooks to copy the shrimp at rest. All should be well weighted to fish close to the bottom. Before the advent of bead-head bugs, shrimp patterns were often the only way of catching deep lying grayling on the fly. They are still very effective. However, ever since it produced a catch of about eighty grayling, my favoured pattern incorporates an orange bead in the centre of the body to copy the orange blob of the parasite.

MIDGES

Midges emerge from their eggs as larvae and mostly remain in the mud, weed or moss, only occasionally rising to the surface. Most larvae are olive-green but at least one species (commonly known as the bloodworm) is red because of the amounts of haemoglobin in its body. So far as the

[22] *Ecology*, vol 78, pp 1098–1104, reported in *BBC Wildlife Magazine*, September, 1997

grayling fisher is concerned, imitating the behaviour of the natural larvae is extremely difficult. Their movement is a strange lashing motion which propels them through the water. It is possible to imitate this when still-water fishing, but it is impossible to imitate this movement in flowing water. The larva changes into a slow-swimming pupa and when the adult is ready to emerge the pupae ascend to the surface. Depending upon the air temperature the pupae hang in the surface film for a while and at this stage, and as an adult on the surface they can be imitated by the fly fisher. It is common on slow moving lengths of river for grayling to be found leisurely sipping at the pupae hanging in the film. On slow water the meniscus is thicker and any accumulated surface scum makes the emergence of the adult midge much slower.

Midge pupae have been much overlooked in river fly fishing but in recent years the value of their imitation has been recognised. Some good use has been made of the stillwater pupa imitations but I think that the more intricate detail of some of these patterns is wasted. I have found that simple imitations emphasising the colour, size and shape of the pupa are best. Two patterns, the Culard and a very small black emerger based on a tiny Klinkhamer stand out for dimpling grayling, whether they are taking midges, smuts or some small terrestrial fly.

Except in calmer water, grayling often take midge pupae in such a way that the visible evidence of feeding may be missed. The grayling's rise to these flies in the film is a mere kiss of the surface, a tiny disturbance of a very small area. My favourite pattern in these circumstances has changed over the years. For the last few seasons I have used the Masham Midge, which rests flush on the surface. It is really a dry fly fished damp and not a strict imitation of the pupa. The Masham Midge is named after the stretch of the River Ure that I've fished for the last ten years; the same part of the river for which Tom Sturdy devised his Sturdy's Fancy. The river has a large population of grayling. It is probably Yorkshire's most prolific grayling river although I have yet to catch a two-pounder from it. It is in the slower stretches that grayling are found leisurely taking midges, reed smuts and small terrestrials. When grayling rise to these tiny flies I find it impossible to get any indication of their size; for example, I have caught grayling between ten and forty centimetres from the same area without a clue as to their size until the hook set. Big grayling can rise to tiny food in the film with less disturbance than an aggressive minnow. Never overlook a small rise unless you know it is from a small fish. Sometimes small grayling can be splashy risers and one soon learns to be aware of them. Much more difficult are the angel's kisses, the merest dimples which might be one of the recent spring's new generation or a potential record breaker. I have learned to my cost, but become much wiser because of it, how big grayling can take flies from the film in the most subtle way. Too often in the learning process I chose to ignore the tiny rises in the backwaters or well to the side of the current or in the shallows as I concentrated on the fish activity in the main stream. It was only as I waded closer and spooked the fish or I took a closer look on exiting the river and viewing from the vantage of the bank that I learned the truth that grayling of all sizes mix together and may rise without any indication of their size.

TERRESTRIALS

I was quite surprised to find that terrestrial aerial insects featured so highly in Dr Woolland's survey of River Dee grayling – 25% by number. Terrestrials occurred in slightly less than half the fish examined, thus those grayling which fed on them did so keenly; in fact, on average, terrestrials represented half their intake. Excluding the months of January, February and March, River Dee grayling take more terrestrials than any other food item although caddis larvae remain the leader by volume. And for the angler, frequency of occurrence is paramount. Significantly for the dry-fly angler, aerial terrestrials were more than twice as important as aerial aquatic flies. The total of duns, spinners, adult stoneflies, midges and adult sedges came to less than 10% by number. Not suprisingly, the highest consumption of terrestrials occurred in heavily wooded parts of the river. Terrestrial insect consumption was highest in the May to October period, but November, December and April were also important months. All rivers are unique, but the feeding patterns of the Dee must have significance for similar British rivers. Whether or not you are impressed by surveys of grayling stomach contents, be aware of the possibilities on offer. The menu selection is rarely entirely aquatic. Often it is mixed and there may be just a few times when it is solely terrestrial.

The obvious lies where terrestrials will be most available to grayling are close to trees and overhanging bushes and downstream of these areas. On small rivers and streams with plenty of bankside foliage terrestrials will feature more prominently than on wider rivers. Windy days will ensure that more insects find their way onto the surface. If you find yourself puzzling over grayling rising mid-river and a hundred yards from the nearest trees or bushes it may still be to a steady supply of terrestrials.

When using terrestrial patterns I have caught many more trout than grayling. Why ? Because at least until early summer I concentrate on trout and save grayling fishing for midsummer when on my rivers they are fully fit. I find that grayling are not so catholic in their selection of terrestrials as trout, which may take anything from the tiny aphid to a large cranefly. Small beetles, ants, black gnats and aphid imitations work best.

Most of my terrestrial patterns are fished dry in the conventional manner although I am becoming impressed with the wet Killer Beetle. I sometimes wonder whether beetle imitations fished wet are also taken for snails, which on some streams, especially the chalk streams, figure highly in grayling diets[23]. The general shape and colour of black beetle patterns such as Eric's Beetle and the Coch-y-bondhu are fair imitations of black snails. Fished close to the river bed or weeds, I'm sure the wet beetle pattern doubles its value as an imitation.

The Killer Beetle is becoming a popular fly for grayling and trout on the Ure and other northern rivers. It is usually fished as a trailing fly behind a larger pattern. Tie it onto the bend of the hook on about twelve inches (30 cm) of about two pounds b.s. mono. The weighted trailing beetle sinks. It attracts grayling in its own right but I suspect it also catches fish that inspected and refused the dry fly. Takes are revealed by a swirl in the water or a pause or movement of the dry fly. Peter Welsh, the creator of the fly, in addition to fishing it as a single fly or in tandem behind a dry fly, also fishes it as a trailing fly behind a goldhead. Peter noticed that when grayling become suspicious of a goldhead they will often take the small beetle in its wake. The smaller, more natural pattern succeeds where the too familiar or ambiguous goldhead arouses only a sceptical examination.

From midsummer until the end of autumn, small green aphids are very common on trees and grasses. They often fall onto the river surface and end up as fish food. When grayling take them it is invariably on slow-moving water and the rise form is a dainty sip.Good aphid imitations are

[23] Survey published in *Trout and Grayling, An Angler's Natural History* (A & C Black), 1979, by Norman Maclean

easy to tie. The more difficult part is the natural presentation of such a small fly. Small flies demand fine, soft tippets. The last few inches of tippet should sink and definitely not float. When using size 18 hooks and smaller, the ratio of grayling hooked to those risen can be very disappointing. I regard hooking one in three as pretty good. If the fish are small the ratio will be greater.

REED SMUTS (Simulium spp.)

I suspect that smuts have an importance for grayling out of all proportion to their tiny size. Fly fishermen usually encounter reed smuts on warm summer days when trout and grayling seem to be preoccupied with them. But not all of the nineteen species emerge at the same time of year. Some appear as late as November and others as early as February, although in much fewer numbers than in the summer. The type of water they prefer varies between species with many favouring fast flowing water with a gravel base. Others are found in water of a more moderate pace with a good weed growth. The larvae are a grey or creamy-white colour and are only about a quarter of an inch (6–7 mm) long. They have a small sucker at the posterior by which they cling to weeds, rocks or other object on the riverbed. Grayling feed on them by grazing off weeds and stones. The larvae are easily alarmed and if disturbed will release their grip and drift freely downstream where they are eagerly devoured by trout and grayling. This is a very difficult food to imitate with the fly.

The larvae pupate prior to hatching at the surface. There is a build up of gas beneath the skin of the pupa and this tiny bubble helps it rise to the surface. The winged fly, which usually has a black or dark brown body, emerges perfectly dry from its pupal skin. The adult does not need to wait on the surface to dry its wings as ephemeroptera do. Therefore, grayling rarely take the adult fly but rather they concentrate on the pupa hanging in or just below the surface film. The rise form and grayling behaviour generally towards these flies is very similar to that towards midge pupae and the way of fishing the imitation is identical. A useful pattern is Mottram's Smut, to which I add a tiny tip of silver tinsel to help represent the gas within the pupa. I cast it up and across just below the surface on a very fine point in a natural drift.

The broad transparent wings of the adults lay flat over the back when at rest, as with all members of the Diptera order. The adults are very small, most approximately three to four millimetres in length. When, although rarely encountered, the adults are available, the Masham Midge, Culard, Goddard's Smut and small black parachutes are suitable patterns. As with all small flies, it is the twin problems of presentation and hooking that cause the biggest headache.

STONEFLIES (Plecoptera)

On many rivers, especially the fast flowing ones in the North of England, Scotland and the Midlands, stoneflies are of some importance. Conversely, in the chalk streams, only the willow fly is of interest. In northern latitudes outside of Britain, in such places as Canada, Scandinavia and northern Europe, they are a primary food source. Stoneflies prefer fast-flowing rivers with a stony, rocky or gravel bed and stable water temperatures. They are intolerant of pollution and require high oxygen levels.

There may be as many as 3000 species worldwide but about only one tenth of the 300 or more European species are found in the UK. The British species vary considerably in size, from the adult needle fly, a mere 5–9 mm body length, to the large stoneflies which may reach a length of 24 mm (one inch) and have a wingspan of about 50 mm.

The nymphs have a head with two antennae, and three thoracic segments and ten abdominal segments. They have two tails, which is the easiest way to differentiate them from British upwing (ephemeroptera) nymphs which all have three. Most spend about a year in the nymphal stage but some larger species may take three years to hatch. As maturity approaches, the wing pads darken and eventually the nymphs crawl to dry land to split their nymphal skins and emerge as winged adults. The shoreward migration is not the quick swimming ascent of ephemeroptera, but a slow crawl. In the weeks before emergence they become more active, which exposes them to increased predation. When summer fishing I sometimes use a large or medium weighted stonefly nymph on the point to fish close to river bed. It catches its fair share of trout but very few grayling[24]. I can offer no explanation.

[24] Paul Marriner comments that when in the North West Territories, Canada, he used large golden stonefly imitations (size 2, 4XL) during high and dirty water conditions; they were exceedingly effective!

The adults have two tails and hard shiny wings. The wings at rest are flat along the top of the abdomen. The needle-flies, as their name suggests, are extremely thin. Most species are various shades of brown with the exception of the yellowish-green Yellow Sally. The males of many species the wings have mere stubs for wings, thus flight is impossible and mating takes place on the ground. The adults stay in the vicinity of the river, in trees and in the undergrowth and rarely will they be found, unlike ephemeroptera, far from the water. The egg-laying females return to the river after a few days to oviposit on the surface. This they do in a number of ways; by dipping repeatedly their abdomens, or by a single landing and stationary release, or by dragging their dipped abdomens in the film as they skitter across the surface. Trout and grayling feed on these females but I have only seen the smaller stoneflies ovipositing. In October it is not unusual to find the female willow and needle flies ovipositing and afterwards to see them spent, with their four wings spread star-like on the surface. Grayling rise freely to them and an imitation of the small dry stonefly should bring success. Oliver Edwards ties a superb spent imitation for grayling, what he terms 'a real October special'.

Several North Country spider patterns from the nineteenth century and earlier, have traditionally been fished as stonefly imitations. The Light Woodcock, Partridge and Orange, Winter Brown, Early Brown and Needle flies are examples. These patterns are presented just below the surface, never much deeper than a few inches. Stonefly nymphs are rarely found in the upper water levels. The nymphs are poor swimmers and stay close to the stream bed. So why should these spiders, fished as stoneflies be representing a natural so close to the surface ? The only explanations are that they represent drowned spent ovipositing females or both male and female adults who being poor fliers and never venture far from the river, when at the mercy of the wind sometimes are blown onto the surface. Under the rippling water they soon drown and are submerged. Even if this happens infrequently it occurs often enough to make the artificials acceptable throughout the season.

UPWING OR MAYLIES (Ephemeroptera)

When the mature nymphs of the ephemeroptera swim in open water or are dislodged from their habitats of weed, moss or the surface of stones, they soon become grayling food. Likewise, the adult duns on the surface and the female egg-laying spinners are consumed broadly in proportion to their availability. On most alkaline streams the majority of the nymphs are the slim, agile-darting or moss-creeping types plus the burrowing Mayflies. Elsewhere and on most other grayling rivers the flat stone-clinging nymphs are also important.

Although the size and shape of the various nymph types are quite different, the basic physiology is the same. They all have ten abdominal segments with gills, three thoracic segments, a head, six legs, two antennae and three tails. (A few European and American species have two tails.) It is fairly easy to tell one nymph type from another after just a glance; the body shape alone is usually sufficient.

Traditionally, most nymph fishing involved imitating the agile-darting species, mainly of the Baetis family. They abound in all grayling rivers but particularly in the weedy chalk streams. Agile-darters are strong swimmers capable of moving in and out of their microhabitat. Although many are quite small, even at maturity, they are often found in substantial numbers. It is this frequency combined with high activity that stimulates grayling and trout attention. For these reasons they can be reliably imitated by the fly fisher at any time.The flat stone-clinging species common to all stony rivers are much poorer swimmers and never venture beyond their localised habitat except to migrate to the surface or when they enter the drift to move. Their flat, broad bodies and strong legs enables them to cling tightly to flat stones and rapidly crawl away from predators.

Nymphs grow by a series of moults until the time is right for emergence. The wing pads enlarge and often darken during the final instar. Most nymphs swim to the surface; some merely float with little body movement, others like the stone-clingers wobble or flutter slightly in their ascent and still others with a jerky, undulating movement. A very few species emerge below the surface or crawl up rocks etc in the margins to emerge. It is the final emergence ascent that attracts grayling attention.

As for the imitation of nymphs I am sure that size and shape are the key features. Colouring and movement are less important. Most of my nymph-caught grayling come to a naturally-drifted imitation. Of course there are times when I will work a nymph, ie, retrieve it faster than the current or lift in the manner of a rising natural.

Once at the surface, as the nymph rests against the meniscus, the upper side of the thoracic skin splits, then the skin over the head splits and the winged adult, the dun, begins to emerge from the nymphal skin and push through the surface film. Some photographs of this emergence show the thoracic split as opening a hole in the meniscus so that the adult emerges dry. Initially the wings are a crumpled clump which are erected as blood is pumped through the veins. The abdomen is pulled free of the nymphal shuck and the dun finds itself on the dry side of the surface film where it is able to fully erect its wings and dry them before taking flight. A lot of nymphs and duns don't fulfil the mission. They die in the process of shedding the skin or become trapped by the surface tension. All emergers are an attractive grayling food and I find that during a hatch of duns, patterns fished low in the film are more effective than conventional dun imitations. They succeed because emerger patterns represent an easier target for feeding fish. The fly is not copying a dun about to leave the surface but the insect struggling or trapped in the film.

The duns are the first of a two stage adult. All have upright wings, six legs, a segmented body and two or three tails. Most are sombrely coloured. Their imitation is considered in a later chapter. After taking flight they will head towards vegetation, where, usually within forty-eight hours, the thoracic skin splits and they complete the transformation from dun to spinner. In comparison to the duns, the spinners have longer tails and legs, the body is brighter and the wings shiny, transparent and more heavily veined. Reproduction occurs in flight, often in the evening, and the females return to the water to oviposit. The egg ball at the rear of the abdomen is clearly visible on some species. Spinners are an insignificant part of the total grayling diet, but when they are on the water they can represent one hundred percent of what is being taken. Being caught without a suitable imitation usually means remaining fishless. To be precise, it is the spent spinner, rather than one in the act of egg-laying, that is most attractive to fish. The egg-layers dip their abdomens below the surface either when resting on the water or in flight, and some return to the surface a number of times. Some Baetis species crawl below the surface to oviposit and get eaten when trying to swim back to the surface. Spent spinners lying flush in the film are easy pickings for grayling and trout. A leisurely rise, sometimes barely breaking the surface is indicative of spinners being taken.

Some of my most intense periods of dry-fly fishing for grayling in recent years have been during spinner falls towards the end of a summer evening. Sedge hatches prompt similar gluttony. But the grayling reaction to spinners is less like a group of ten year old boys let loose in a sweet shop, more a lazy dinner party where the diners casually pick and choose from a vast buffet laid before them.

Occasionally the spinner clouds can be vast, like an Egyptian plague, hovering over the river before dropping to the surface. Principally, these large spinner falls occur in the summer, not the traditional grayling season. Thus they have been overlooked. However, my fishing records reveal some excellent catches, including some large specimens, when spinners are on the water. The imitation should always be fished flush in the film and dead drift. In the failing light these are often very difficult to see and one can do no more than watch for a rise in the general area the fly should be in. Inevitably you end up striking at rises to naturals and also missing some of the real takes because the fly cannot be tracked accurately.

Composition of the Diet of R. Dee Grayling by % Number, Volume and Occurrence

	% Number	% Volume	% Occurrence
Ephemeropteran nymphs	**8.5**	**5.9**	**48.8**
Baetis spp.	2.0	1.0	46.0
Ephemerella ignita	5.0	3.7	26.0
Others	1.5	1.2	9.7
Ephemeropteran adults	**4.5**	**3.7**	**29.5**
Plecopteran nymphs	**8.6**	**4.2**	**51.1**
Chloroperla torrentium	4.6	1.6	34.1
Isoperla grammatica	1.8	1.3	23.6
Others	2.2	1.3	9.0
Plecopteran adults	**1.7**	**1.5**	**17.1**
Trichopteran larvae	**20.0**	**49.7**	**92.5**
cased larvae	*15.1*	*44.4*	*78.8*
Potomophylax latipennis	1.2	15.8	21.7
Glossoma conformis	1.8	8.4	14.4
Goera pilosa	0.6	4.9	10.9
Others	11.5	15.3	33.6
uncased caddis	*4.9*	*5.3*	*57.4*
Hydropsyche instabilis	4.3	4.5	51.6
Others	0.6	0.8	12.9
Trichopteran adults	**0.3**	**0.8**	**12.2**
Dipteran larvae	**14.4**	**4.5**	**80.3**

(*continued*)

	% Number	% Volume	% Occurrence
Dipteran pupae	**2.1**	**0.5**	**17.0**
Dipteran adults	**2.0**	**0.6**	**19.7**
Mollusca	**2.4**	**2.2**	**26.9**
Ancylastrum fluviatile	2.2	1.8	20.2
Others	0.2	0.4	4.4
Crustacea	**5.9**	**5.4**	**34.6**
Asellus meridianus	4.5	3.0	29.0
Gammarus pulex	1.4	2.4	16.1
Terrestrial aerial insects	**25.1**	**14.4**	**46.9**
Coleoptera	**2.8**	**2.2**	**47.4**
Arachnida	**1.1**	**0.1**	**20.2**
Corixidae	**0.2**	**0.2**	**10.0**
Megaloptera	**0.1**	**0.3**	**6.3**
Hirudinea	**0.1**	**0.2**	**5.4**
Fish	*** **0.1**	**0.3**	**1.7**
Other items	**0.2**	**0.8**	**2.5**

Table I

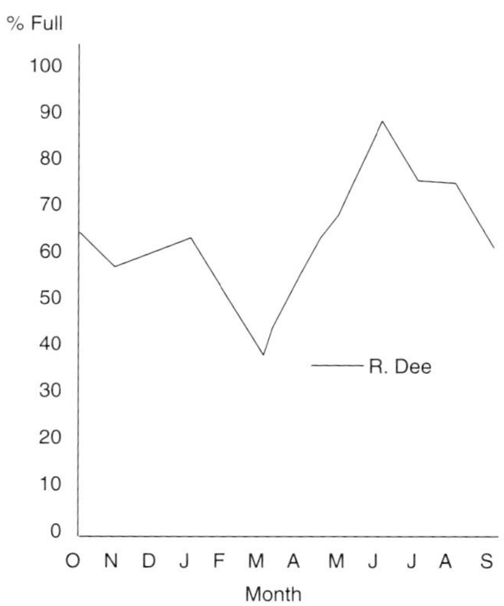

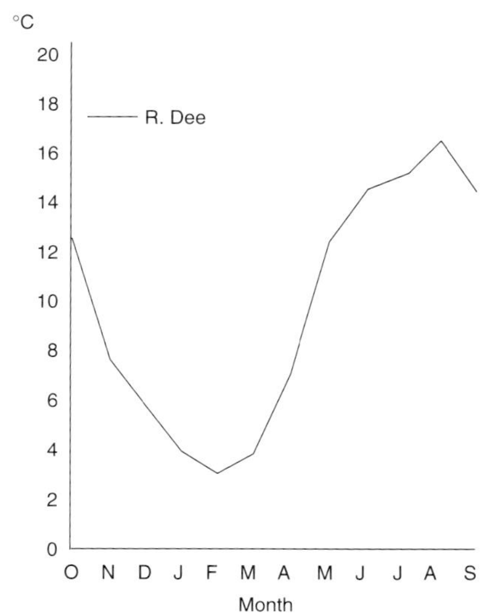

Water Temperatures

Seasonal variation in stomach fullness

4

Fly Fishing Methods

'Moreover, the angler may fish dry or wet, casting upstream, downstream or across. Indeed, so many are the possible methods of using the fly, and so many the enthusiastic specialists in this, that or the other mode, that, with apologies to Kipling I am tempted to write:

> Here is wisdom for your use.
> So do not, I pray, refuse
> To accept the mighty truths experts attest.
> Twenty ways do angers try
> To present the grayling fly,
> And every blessed one of them is best.'

W. Carter Platts, *Grayling Fishing* (1939)

LITTLE HAS CHANGED SINCE W. Carter Platts wrote those words, rather we have added to the variety of fly fishing methods and patterns in use. Today there is a much wider choice in the way we fly fish for grayling than existed sixty years ago. I would never suggest that one style is better than another. One might be a more effective method at a given time, but numbers are not the only reason we go grayling fishing. I fish the way I do because it gives me the most pleasure. I get great satisfaction from being an adaptable angler, i.e., changing methods and patterns until finding the combination that matches the fish's feeding patterns. That is where my pleasure is derived. I know a few fly fishers who dote on the dry fly and wouldn't dream of owning a weighted braided leader; yet there are others for whom the dry fly takes less than ten percent of their fishing time. Perhaps a team of three spider patterns is the first choice for one angler, but another may fish a weighted bug all season. There never will be a correct way, just one that gives you the most satisfaction.

Much of the grayling fly fishing tradition in the U.K. involves the subsurface fly rather than the dry fly. I believe this is so because of the customary restriction to autumn and winter fishing. Had our predecessors turned their attention to grayling three months earlier when there are more duns, spinners, caddis and terrestrial flies, it's likely the list of grayling dry flies would be longer. As it is, the flies we know specifically as grayling flies are mainly in the fancy category. This is because, quite rightly, imitations of the natural fly are equally as effective for both trout and grayling, but the latter, with their weakness for a flash of colour, have afforded the inventive tier the opportunity to produce flies specially for grayling. Perhaps, autumn and winter grayling respond to 'fancy' patterns because of the scarcity of natural insects, and they're hungry. Conversely, trout at this time feed much less actively.

I am certain that in the last twenty years we have become better grayling anglers, by 'better', I mean more efficient. I also believe that within my circle of grayling fishing friends the larger grayling are being caught more frequently. I attribute this increase in numbers to the developments in grayling fishing techniques and patterns. Grayling are essentially bottom feeders, and the older they are the more they feed there. Ergo, big fish rise to the surface infrequently. It is significant that in the last twenty years we have developed patterns for fishing deep, and the means of delivering them. Previously, the only way to present flies or bait in deep or fast water was under a float. Consequently, it was usually the bait fisherman trotting a brandling or maggot that landed the biggest fish. Now we can get fly patterns down to where grayling will take them. The introduction of heavy beads to the heads of nymphs and bugs has radically altered river fly fishing. Weighted braided leaders to ensure deep presentation and weighted caddis larvae patterns have opened up new areas of the river bed which went largely unfished by fly fishermen. We simply did not have the appropriate patterns or the means of fishing them. Further, the Eastern European nymph fishing style has provided even more opportunities.

Dry-fly anglers have been similarly aided by the development of high strength, low diameter monofilament. For when grayling demand small dry flies, the finer and softer the tippet the better. Now we can fish the smallest dry flies with an acceptable presentation. There is little fear of breakage, except on a sudden strike, as grayling rarely head for weed or obstructions.

Some of the patterns and fishing styles developed in recent years may be an innovation too far for some traditionally minded fly fishers. The heavier nymph and bug methods may not appeal to all grayling anglers, some of whom may be thinking 'Do I need a grayling this badly?' The answer is that they probably don't. The same question is faced by the trout fly fisher too. But the methods and patterns are there if we want them, and if they are appropriate for the rivers we fish. Everyone will develop their own preferences in fly fishing; mine is definitely for dry-fly fishing but I am a realist. If I want to maximise my time on the river and catch more fish than I would by a single method I must adapt. Just how far one is prepared to adapt to patterns and methods that explore the boundaries of fly fishing is down to personal preference.

DRY FLY FISHING

'In fly-fishing for grayling it is a very frequent occurrence to rise a fish three or four times, missing him on every occasion, but basketing him after all. Now in the case of a trout it is seldom that this happens, so I consider the grayling a more sociable fish than his speckled comrade, and less easily alarmed.' Francis Walbran, *British Angler* (1889)

For all that grayling take most of their food from the stream bed they are extremely cooperative with the dry-fly fisherman. All my Lapland grayling over two pounds took a dryish pattern and many of the better grayling from my home rivers were tempted to the surface. Generally speaking, I prefer to fish dry, whether for trout or grayling, and fortunately from early summer until the end of October grayling are free risers. From November onwards it may take a hatch of fly or some persistence to entice them to the top. Regardless, at this time dry fly is less reliable than subsurface presentations. While it is very possible to fish in

January and February with a floating fly I have found that the necessary conditions are clear water, warm sunshine and some aquatic fly activity.

Sometimes grayling will rise with reckless abandon, much more so than wild trout. At other times they stay locked in their lies close to the bottom. What motivates the rise is a fly hatch or food arriving on the river, such as terrestrials or egg-laying flies. Sometimes grayling are not particularly fastidious about the choice of fly or the manner in which it is presented. But the contrast is so marked between their audacity one day, and their canny circumspection on another that you could believe you were fishing for two different species. Once autumn has begun I find them far less predictable. Trout, under a given set of circumstances, usually behave in certain ways, but this enigmatic cousin may be every bit a lady in her whims and preferences. She can be seduced by a flash of colour, or some glittering gold may win her round to your way of thinking. She may be capricious in what keeps her happy, for where one day she was satisfied with a diet of iron blues, the next, only be tempted by a bright concoction of bead and fur that would make a brown trout bolt for cover.

This unpredictability is not restricted to the dry fly or surface feeding but it is a common characteristic of grayling disposition towards all artificial flies and towards feeding generally. Grayling that show no interest in either natural food or an artificial fly may suddenly, without obvious cause or reason, start to feed or respond to the artificial. Equally, they may well decide to stop just as abruptly. If grayling can be found, and even if unresponsive I would stick with them. Certainly try out a range of patterns to stimulate some response but if you have no luck then give them a rest for ten minutes. That may be all it takes for them to start feeding. Except for the early months of the year, grayling are invariably cooperative at some stage of the day.

For everyone who believes that the size or pattern of fly is critical, and that a grayling's scrutiny in this matter is second to none, I relate a simple illustration of grayling fickleness. Hans and Ina van Klinken and I were fishing the River Ure which was at a high summer level and rising. The only steadily rising fish we could find were in the slower water and only then in the late afternoon, in the margins under a tree-lined bank. Hans was regularly catching a mixture of trout and grayling under these very unfavourable circumstances. Ina and I had struggled to catch a few fish but Hans has psychokinetic skill at extracting grayling. He changed flies regularly, partially to experiment but also to find a consistently acceptable pattern. One individual grayling rose to a succession of flies, from a size 18 Culard to a size 8 Klinkhamer, the latter tied on the very large Partridge K12ST hook. The body length of the Culard was about six millimetres and the Klinkhamer's approximately forty millimetres. This proves nothing, except that grayling can be either careless or selective in their choice of acceptable patterns. From the way they tolerated the wide range of flies you could think them easily caught, but Hans had to work hard for those fish. I must assume that in this instance presentation was all important.

Grayling activity on the surface does not necessarily mean that they are going to be easy to catch; their erratic and inconsistent attitude about whether they defer to the dry fly can lead to great frustration. Nine times out of ten rising grayling will respond to a well presented artificial, but on the tenth they cause far more humiliation than trout.

Summer grayling are not the soft option for the frustrated trout angler. Some of the most difficult rising grayling I have encountered have been on the middle Wharfe in summer. During the late evening, the blue-winged olive hatches and the returning spinners can mean great numbers of flies on the surface. At times I have seen the pools alive with rising grayling, but despite their voracious appetites and the dwindling light, I have risen embarrassingly few. I still have no satisfactory answer. The more common frustration occurs when grayling rise to the tiniest surface flies, which are almost invisible to our eye. These are probably smuts in, rather than on the meniscus. When this happens, my friend Bernard Benson regularly sieves the river surface with a small-mesh net, only to find nothing in it but what he most aptly calls 'biro dots'. Grayling take these minuscule insects all season and offer a challenge to the most skilful fly fisherman. I have encountered many surface-feeding summer grayling which were far more difficult than the trout alongside them.

THE KLINKHAMER SPECIAL

As I check through my fishing diary, in which is recorded every fishing trip I have made since 1976, I can assess which flies have worked best for me. Since 1988 one fly has been outstandingly successful – the Klinkhamer Special; it has revolutionised my grayling and trout fishing. When I first used it I must have been among a mere handful of British anglers who had seen it work. Now I doubt if there is a serious grayling fly fisher in Europe who hasn't tried it.

Hans van Klinken and I had corresponded about grayling and we met for the first time at the Dutch Fly Fair in 1988. Immediately after the fair we fished together on the River Kyll in Germany where I was introduced to two of Hans' patterns. Both the Klinkhamer Special and the Leadhead Nymph proved dramatically successful on that three-day trip. At the time, in accordance with grayling tradition my boxes held only very small flies. Perhaps my largest was a size 12 Little Red Sedge or a size 12 Dove Bug or Killer Bug but the majority of my dry flies were tied on size 16 or 18 hooks. Hans was using, and quickly persuaded me to use, his large dry flies and inch-long nymphs. I remember Hans showing me his fly box and thinking that he wouldn't get me using those! After half an hour's fruitless fishing while Hans had caught half a dozen, his wife, Ina came down the river bank bringing samples of Hans' flies to try for myself. I have never looked back.

How and why Hans devised the Klinkhamer Special in 1985 has been documented elsewhere[1]. It was tied originally for Norwegian grayling in fast water and Hans declared the fly to be an emerging caddis. Whatever its pedigree, it does not matter. What it is today is the best fast water grayling and trout dry fly in the world. That is only my opinion but I've thought long enough before committing myself. Of course I haven't fished it all over the world, but I correspond with fly fishers on five continents who do, and they, like everyone else to whom I've recommended the fly, cannot praise it more highly. I have fished it in Canada, central Europe, Lapland and in the UK, and found it to be the most exceptional pattern I have come across. Sceptical hosts in various countries have looked on in amazement as local flies failed and my claims to having the answer proved justified. Just last season, I was surprised to find two river fly fishers who had not heard of the fly. As I exited the River Tweed on the last day of the trout season, having caught a mixed bag of about two dozen trout and grayling to seventeen inches, I spread the Klinkhamer gospel to two fishless anglers. Having watched my previous half hour's frantic activity in amazement, they were eager listeners. I guaranteed

[1] *The World's Best Trout Flies* 1994 edited by John Roberts and the *Journal of the Grayling Society* Autumn 1987

them a better season next year as they gratefully cradled samples of their new wonder fly. There may be better flies for a specific job, such as the Killer Bug or the Pheasant Tail nymph for grayling on the chalk streams, but for both trout and grayling at the heads of freestone pools and in riffles across the world, from the first day of the season until the last, from dawn until dusk, the Klinkhamer is outstanding. Since I was introduced to the fly I have tried to give it as much publicity as possible, believing that good news is for sharing. Thankfully, Hans has not adopted the attitude of some tiers who attempt to patent a pattern or tying style. He is a generous, gregarious man who would rather give away a successful fly than try to surround it in secrecy or make money from it. Worldwide, it will become as important a fly as Lee Wulff's series of dry flies or Frank Sawyer's Pheasant Tail, and it has deservedly given Hans some fly-fishing immortality.

The Klinkhamer must be prepared correctly for the best results. It is important that the abdomen and thorax are treated with an appropriate material to ensure they sink below the surface. The hackle and wing should be treated with floatant.

It was only after using some of Hans' patterns that I became aware of how far grayling will lie towards the head of a pool or riffle. In recent years my biggest grayling have been caught in these areas which previously I often passed by. Unfortunately, I cannot match Hans' 2.2 kg, sixty one centimetre grayling that fell to a Klinkhamer.

Grayling resting in a depression on the stream bed and out of the current, are prepared to cross four or five feet of fast water to intercept the Klinkhamer. I have fished it on the River Kaitum in Swedish Lapland in fast, boulder strewn water of considerable depth, perhaps eight feet or more in some pools, and grayling have risen from the bottom and crossed the powerful water flow to take this fly. A depth of four feet on the Wharfe, Tweed or Dee is as nothing when this is on the menu.

The secret of the fly's success is the long abdomen hanging below the surface. The broad parachute hackle attracts some attention, but it is the emerger-like body hanging tantalisingly below the surface that is an irresistible magnet for trout and grayling. Although it was devised for use during a caddis hatch, I find that it is very useful when there is nothing or little rising. Whether I am trout fishing in April, midsummer grayling and trout fishing, or autumn fishing just for grayling, I fish it in the faster water in the top half of a pool. It also works in the slower water further down a pool, but it is not quite so effective. There is no better dry fly for the riffles or for rocky pocket water. Fish have to make their minds up quickly about food passing swiftly overhead and they take it with enthusiasm. While they usually come up and hit it hard, both trout and grayling may jump out of the water and land on it, or they may simply grab the tip of the abdomen and pull the fly through the film without any disturbance at all. Grayling take in all three ways but the last is the one catches you unawares. This is why the large visible, white poly yarn wing is so important, at least to the angler, it makes no difference to the fish. I have used different coloured wings without any noticeable effect, and at dusk I use a pink poly yarn wing for better visibility.

There are many stretches of rocky riffle on the Ure which in summer may be no more than shin deep with depressions adding another few inches. The rippled surface hides the fish and gives them the impression of cover above. There, one July afternoon, I caught four grayling, between one and half to one and three-quarter pounds on the Klinkhamer.These are good grayling in any river but they were notable because they were the only fish I caught in a two hour period. They were all larger than average fish, and were in shallow water. Not only did it prove the effectiveness of the Klinkhamer, but it emphasised how even shallow fast water, especially in summer temperatures, will hold grayling.

When the fly is taken out of the context of a caddis hatch, when it is fished as a search pattern, what do fish take it for? Perhaps they still see the emerging caddis in it and respond, or perhaps it is just the sight of something big and obviously food-like hanging below the surface that does the trick. My good friend, Oliver Edwards has his own, very viable, theory.[2] … 'It is in my view, the way this pattern sits *in* the water which makes it unique and suggestive of a whole host of struggling, half-drowned, juicy insects. It is surely taken for many of the larger terrestrials which fall onto the river every season. … They all kick or vibrate their wings when trapped in the glue-like meniscus – and the meniscus always tends to be thicker during hot weather. Their desperate actions make patterns on the surface and it is my opinion that the Klinkhamer, with its many-fibred parachute hackle, may give a passable impression of one these large struggling terrestrials. In high summer, trout and grayling rely

[2] *Oliver Edwards' Flytyers Masterclass* 1994 by Oliver Edwards

quite heavily on terrestrial food items and, while apparent fasting through the heat of the day seems to occur, it is also well known that, given the opportunity, a good mouthful, feebly kicking and passing directly overhead, is rarely refused.'

In 1998 Hans and I were discussing grayling flies when he said that he had a new, highly successful grayling method that he had not mentioned to anyone. My ears pricked up immediately. It was, in fact, something that I had already discovered, along with probably many other Klinkhamer users. Hans often fishes the Klinkhamer fully submerged and finds it takes fish that haven't wanted to rise. Scores of times over the last decade I have unwittingly allowed a well soaked and grayling-chewed Klinkhamer to descend below the surface, only to discover that a grayling or trout has hooked itself. What they take it for may require some convoluted explanation. Oliver fishes a yellow Klinkhamer as a Yellow May dun emerger and often allows it to sink just below the surface to imitate the emerger, the only stage of the lifecyle when grayling and trout will feed upon the natural. It is another aspect to this versatile fly.

In appropriate colours the fly is also an excellent imitation of an emerging Mayfly. In recent seasons I have enjoyed excellent Mayfly hatches on the Derbyshire Derwent and Wye and the Yorkshire rivers Nidd and Rye. My fishing diary confirms that a daily average of over twenty trout and grayling approved of the Klinkhamer.

In smaller sizes it works very well in slower water and when smaller natural duns are expected. The mini-Klinkhamer is very effective and it has become a much copied style for emerging midges on stillwater. A black mini-Klinkhamer (tied on size 18 Partridge K4A hooks) is excellent when grayling take tiny flies in the film. A larger black version works well when hawthorn flies are on the water.

The Klinkhamer is the ideal fly to use when a lot of mending is required. The bulk of this large fly, seven-eighths submerged like an iceberg acts as a good anchor against which to mend the line and leader. The Klinkhamer rarely moves far even when the line is vigorously rolled.

FISHING THE CADDIS HATCHES

One of my favourite times for fishing is during the late evening of a mild summer day, say from mid-June until mid-August. During these evenings there is frequently an hour or so's frantic feeding by trout and grayling as spinners return and sedges begin to hatch in vast quantities. When the light fails, fish lose their natural caution and in a big hatch they will feed with corybantic recklessness. They chase the ascending pupae to the surface and feed voraciously on those emergers. Every fish in the river seems to be on the feed, including the bigger ones who usually remain deep and are reluctant surface feeders. If big grayling feed less off the top as they grow older, this is the exception when they relive their youth.

In these circumstances I often fish a team of flies, a Klinkhamer and a Superpupa. I have experimented with switching the patterns between the point and the dropper but have come to no conclusion about their relative merits. The Superpupa may be fished dry, in the film or just below the surface. I fish the team in every direction depending upon the geography of the stream and my access to it. I usually fish them with a drag-free presentation, but as the light fades I worry less about this and it is often the dragging fly that gets the most takes. When darkness comes there may be so many rises to natural flies and the light so bad that I cannot make out my flies so I deliberately keep in closer contact with the flies and keep them moving. When fishing upstream I sometimes retrieve them slightly faster than the current; or when fishing across I retrieve them very slowly with a figure of eight so I can feel any takes. When fishing downstream I may simply let them slowly swing below me and wait for the gentle pluck (rare), a firm take (more likely) or a violent wrench (quite common, particularly in fast water). Big grayling may be very aggressive in these situations. Adult sedge patterns will work at these times but they are nowhere near as effective as the pupa or emerger.

I came across the Superpupa at the Tjounajokk fishing camp, located above the Arctic Circle in Swedish Lapland. I was amongst a small party who had arrived that day and we were anxious to start fishing. The time was somewhere between 11 pm and 1 am and the light was just about good enough to tie on a fly. Typically for a sedge hatch, I couldn't see any flies coming off the river but there were intermittent splashes to the pupae. My usual patterns were catching the odd grayling but not in great numbers. I hadn't seen much of the guide who was sticking closely to another guest, Jennifer Smith (now Olsson). My friend and trip organiser Lars-Åke Olsson was also showing more interest in helping a not very distressed damsel than a struggling pal. When I eventually elicited advice from the guide he showed me a nondescript palmered fly at which I promptly turned my nose up. It is a foolish angler who spurns local advice, especially on his first day fifteen hundred miles from home. I learnt my lesson that night and from the following day until to date I have carried Superpupa patterns wherever I have fished, whether on river or stillwater.

I like so many aspects about the pattern. First is that it catches a lot of grayling and trout. Second, its nondescript shape roughly imitates so many aquatic flies and not just an emerging sedge. Third, by varying the colours and sizes it increases its versatility. Finally, it is very easy to tie.

I have now fished the Superpupa widely in Britain and have come to depend upon it. Unless there is a specific hatch of fly on which grayling are feeding, I often include a Superpupa on a dropper when dry-fly fishing. Depending on its colouring it is mistaken for a wide range of emerging flies and terrestrial insects. It is one of the few emerging sedge patterns that I find works on the West Beck, the East Yorkshire chalk stream. In low water conditions the Superpupa has proved to be sufficiently suggestive of something struggling in the film that even surface-shy fish have taken it confidently.

The dry adult sedge imitation is an effective search fly. The Little Red Sedge or a small dark pattern in the Elk Hair style work well. Grayling don't take many naturals because they are not on the water long enough except at egg-laying and this is often after dark. However, they often respond to the imitation during the day. I usually fish the dry adult in a dead drift. If that doesn't work I'll twitch it or give it some sort of movement, particularly if sedges are hatching or returning. This movement draws attention to an artificial lost among the naturals, or simply offers a suggestion of life to a wary grayling.

FANCY OR ATTRACTOR DRY FLIES

Many anglers put great faith in fancy grayling flies throughout the season. I prefer to begin to fish an imitation of what is on or in the water or what could reasonably be expected to be there. If that fails, then I will turn to an attractor pattern.

What do grayling take these fancy flies to be? Patterns that have flashes of red, orange, gold, yellow, silver, green or blue are common, but why are they successful and what makes a fish take one pattern and not another? The answer can only be that grayling see in them something that imitates a natural fly; they are only fancy in that the colours are brighter or gaudier than we would normally associate with the natural flies. Grayling certainly don't take them because they find them pretty, or unusual, or through inquisitiveness, otherwise many other pattern types would be successful. They must represent food, but in a manner to which our eyes are not accustomed. We are conditioned to the olive and dun coloured naturals so we think that a brighter coloured fly, deemed fancy to our eyes, must appear equally and as colourfully conspicuous to grayling. Robin Mulholland[3] put his view like this … 'Herl-bodied flies are successful on the chalk streams just as they are everywhere else. Rolt developed his Witch on the Wylye as both a trout and grayling fly and it is successful there as it is on the Avon. The explanation of the success of such flies as Rolt's Witch, Red Tag, Treacle Parkin, Terry's Terror and the various Bumbles seems to lie in the combination of herl body and bright tag. My conclusion is that this combination … is a good representation of the hatching nymph. The rough body produces the furry effect of occlusion and the bright tag at the red/orange end of the spectrum creates the effect of the haemoglobin in the nymph's body. … Rolt mentions his Witch as being particularly effective close to or under the bank and in rough weather. It may be that fat herl bodies are fair representations of a wide range of miscellaneous insects, some water-borne and some land-borne, which fall on the water particularly on a windy day. I prefer the former explanation, however; it is more logical and has greater appeal than the latter.'

It appears that certain colours, red in particular, are a stimulus in the animal kingdom and grayling seem to confirm the theory. I can think of a couple of dozen grayling flies that have red, crimson or orange in some part of their dressing. All these bright colours, one one can throw in yellow for good measure, appear particularly appealing as a tag. I mentioned in chapter two that male sticklebacks search for parasite-infected shrimp high in carotenoids to enhance their breeding colours. If it is ever proved that grayling react in the same way it would suggest why the red, orange and yellow in the dressing of fancy flies are so effective.

[3] *Grayling – The Fourth Game Fish* 1989 edited by Ron Broughton; chapter 'Grayling in the Chalk Streams' by Robin Mulholland

My own favourite is Terry's Terror which has a combination of yellow and orange in the tag. I believe this increases the pattern's effectiveness. I fish it from midsummer onwards and it is one of the few patterns about which I feel confident when fishing dry beyond the turn of the year. In its larger sizes, 14 and 12, it is said to represent a sedge, although I cannot think why, and in the medium sizes 14 and 16, the olive duns; perhaps the tag gives the impression of an egg-laying spinner. For me it excels in the smallest sizes, 18 and 20. I have fished it widely on northern rivers and on the chalk streams. On the latter it has given me fifty-plus grayling days. This is one of two dry flies that I use on an annual October visit to the Wiltshire Avon where rising grayling find it irresistible. Peter Deane, who was for a long time closely associated with the fly and knew Dr Cecil Terry, its creator, tied it professionally for nearly fifty years from 1948. In my opinion the pattern goes from strength to strength, proving more popular each season. I rate it far higher than the Red Tag with which I have caught relatively few grayling. Peter Deane also considered the Terry's Terror an excellent wet fly. I have lapsed into tying it with a red tag rather than the original orange but it is no less effective. It is best fished on the steady glides but it is also effective in the difficult area at the lip of a pool. Whenever grayling are taking small flies off the surface it is always worth giving a size 18 or smaller Terry's Terror a chance.

Amongst the fancy dry flies, one other is outstanding in my experience. Perhaps because I am fortunate to fish the very waters it was created for, I have used it quite extensively and have found it very effective. Sturdy's Fancy, created by Tom Sturdy for the River Ure in the Masham area, is fancy by name and by the inclusion of an off-white hackle and red tag. But is it just another attractor pattern? Reg Righyni suggested that Sturdy devised the fly for evening fishing when spinners are on the water and it certainly works on the Ure under these circumstances. When egg-laying spinners return in the falling dusk of July and late summer this is a reliable fly for trout and grayling. I fish it into darkness on the steady glides and the calmer water where grayling leisurely mop up spent spinners. It is tied with either a shoulder or parachute hackle, the latter being my preference. Reg rated the fly very highly, although he tied his slightly differently[4] with a close rib of crimson silk to assist the imitation of a spinner. From September onwards it is a good general grayling dry fly. Of

[4] Letter to the author 27.4.84

the shoulder hackled version Reg Righyni wrote … 'I always tie the tags rather on the long side to start off. If the grayling are well on the take, the longer tag helps the fly to float correctly. If the fish are at all choosy, I clip the tag down to size.' I prefer the parachute version because it holds the body on the surface or even in the film, making it more like a spent fly trapped and unable to escape.

DRY FLY PRESENTATION

Imitative dry flies for grayling are the same as those used for trout. Some appropriate dressings are listed in a later chapter. What I would like to discuss here is the style of presentation of the imitation and to consider the consequences, if any, of the fly's design and its presentation.

The grayling pundits of the past, when making their recommendations for dry fly tactics, often stressed the importance of small dry flies that rode high on the water balancing on their hackle tips. In his book *Grayling*, one of the most prominent of such authors, Reg Righyni wrote 'I think it is more important to use a fly that can be seen well by the angler and floats high on the water.' And later '… up on to the hackle points and makes it ride exactly as is wanted.' There was a time when I firmly believed that this was the essential requirement for all dry fly situations. My doubts of a decade ago have led to apostasy. Two areas cause me greatest concern. First, the notion that a fly's body can be supported by the hackle points; second, that this ideal is the best method for grayling.

The high-floating dry fly is a myth. Certainly the body of the conventional, shoulder-hackled fly will not be supported above the surface. The hackle points penetrate the film and allow the body to sink to the surface. Even the stiffest, short-fibred hackles will not help. In fact, in many ways they are worse – the unyielding, stiff fibres penetrate more easily. They are good for drying quickly when false-casting and they look superb. They also allow a dry fly to bounce along a hard surface like a fly-tier's table, but once on water they offer very little support. I tested over twenty shoulder-hackled dry patterns (many with high quality, expensive hackles) by dropping them onto water from a height of eighteen inches, and all rested on their body, with the hackle fibres below the surface. A more successful design for body support is the thorax hackle with a 'V' cut into the lower fibres, but you won't find many patterns tied this way.[5] The upside-down parachute flies[6] of John Goddard and Brian Clarke theoretically offer the best solution, but are fiddly and time-consuming to tie, and awkward to cast accurately.

Small, lightly dressed, shoulder-hackled or even double-hackled flies like the Double Badger and Janus have a proven reputation for grayling – but not necessarily because they are the ideal small dun imitation. A fly with its body in the film copies an emerger, a crippled dun, a terrestrial or a spinner. The natural dun rests on its legs with its thorax supported off the surface, and only the abdomen progressively rests on the meniscus. Grayling have a tiny brain and so may take our imitations without too much scrutiny, including the shoulder-hackled fly.

The majority of grayling I catch on ephemeroptera-imitating dry flies are taken on patterns tied in the paradun style with a parachute hackle situated on top of the body, wound around the base of a single upright wing. Some of the patterns have widely-spaced Microfibbet tails to give good horizontal support but often I don't bother including tails because I've found them irrelevant to success. The paradun style ensures that the body of the fly rests on the surface or in the film or even just below the meniscus. The spread circular hackle supports the body on, in or just under the surface depending upon whether I treat the body with floatant or not. If this is totally contrary to traditional thinking about grayling dry flies then why are the paraduns so successful? They work equally well for trout and grayling, and when the latter have been rising during a hatch, I've not had any trouble with refusals because of the fly's design. I use one basic design which I vary in colour and size. These include a general olive imitation which in different sizes and body shades seems to match many hatches including the pale watery and spurwings. These latter insects are common from May onwards but specially so in September and October at the peak of the grayling dry fly season. I have fished the paraduns in response to dun hatches all over the UK from the Tweed to the Test and grayling have duly responded. The pale watery version is another of the handful of flies which have yielded fifty-plus grayling days. To catch fifty grayling on one dry-fly pattern should be

[5] See Chapter 6, the Gim River Dun

[6] See *The Trout and the Fly* (1980) by John Goddard and Brian Clarke

considered in the perspective that numbers of grayling hooked are a fraction of those that have risen and been missed.

I think the paradun style is much superior to the traditional shoulder hackled dry fly. The shoulder hackle half below the surface is unnatural and misleading but I suspect fish largely ignore it. The paradun is a better representation of a struggling emerger or one trapped in the meniscus. I find that the body length is very important. Fish have a clearer view of the body in the film and an accurate body length is desirable. Most duns are quite small and the artificial's body length should match. I prefer to tie patterns a little shorter as this will be tolerated more than too long a body. The upright wing is easy for the angler to see and gives the grayling a strong image if for some fish the wing is the trigger to the rise.

I reread Roger Woolley's contribution to *The Grayling*[7] as I prepared this book and was surprised, because it was contrary to popular opinion at the time, to find that he too noted: 'There is one peculiarity about the way grayling take dry flies that should be particularly noticed and heeded, and that is that they prefer a dry fly that rides low on the water. Trout prefer a dry fly that rides high and standing up well on its toes, but grayling accept theirs best when low down, even if semi-submerged. ... .' In view of my comments on dry-fly design I have to disagree about trout preferences, but I agree about grayling.

I have mentioned earlier, but it is worth repeating, that grayling change their minds. If trout are predictable, grayling are temperamental. They won't rise one minute, they will the next, and one rise seems the signal to others in shoal. They want a fancy fly, then they don't. If you can find grayling, stick with them because they will feed sooner or later. If they rise for a while and go off, persevere either with a completely different pattern such as a nymph or wet fly, or rest them and try again.

Notwithstanding the Klinkhamer, or the occasional sedge pattern, British grayling prefer small dry flies. The smaller the fly, the more difficult it is to accomplish an acceptable drag-free presentation.The problem is because the fly is attached to the leader, an impediment that has a proportionately greater effect on small flies. Given a free unhindered drift a fair imitation will be taken confidently.The requirement for a small fly, perhaps as small as a size 20 or 22, is often combined with other factors

[7] *The Grayling* by Richard Lake, second edition 1946 with chapters by Roger Woolley

that make the presentation more difficult. From midsummer many rain-fed rivers are often at their lowest and clearest, and the chalk streams in autumn reach their lowest levels. When this coincides with a hatch of fly on a bright sunny day, especially in shallow water, grayling can be very fussy about standards of presentation. Our handicap has lessened in recent years with the introduction of limp, fine diameter, high strength monofilament, but we don't have all the answers.

Hooking grayling on these small flies is more difficult than persuading them to rise in the first place. Often it is a matter of not timing the strike correctly and I firmly believe that the faster my reactions the better. Other times it is quite possible to believe that grayling actually miss the fly. This has been attributed in the past to extraordinary vision on the grayling's part; it turns away at the last moment due to some failure in the presentation or dressing. There is no evidence that grayling have an optical advantage over trout in this respect. It has been suggested that they have poorer eyesight and having risen from the bottom at speed they miss these small flies. Their misjudgement due to a rapid ascent to intercept a moving fly is more plausible to me. However, a friend of mine, Bernard Benson, a very experienced dry-fly fisherman for grayling, has his own theory for grayling rising in medium to fast, to very fast water. His fishing partner, Oliver Edwards, describes it thus[8]: 'Grayling, as we all know, are not designed for taking surface food. Their protruding upper lip makes them better suited to bottom feeding, even though they do regularly rise to flies on the surface. When rising to conventional dry flies, they charge up from the stream bed, dropping back with the current and tilting backwards – past the vertical – as they near the surface. This backward tilt is essential because of the fish's prominent upper lip.

'As the grayling's mouth approaches the fly, a tiny pressure front is pushed ahead (remember the grayling is coming up at speed). Its lips open only at the instant the meniscus is reached by which time the pressure front has developed into a small raised mound of water immediately underneath the dry fly. The dry fly, of course, is tethered to the end of your leader. So, as the pressure mound rises, the dry fly slides away, down this tiny bank of water. The angler reacts instantly to the rise, but there is no resistance – another missed fish.' Bernard is a grayling dry-fly angler

[8] *Oliver Edwards' Flytyers Masterclass* 1994 by Oliver Edwards

of great experience. It is with very good reason that his favourite grayling patterns are the Klinkhamer and the Paradun.

Bernard's theory appears feasible to me. The problem is worse when using small flies because they are more easily deflected. It is also evident when using shoulder-hackled conventional dry flies, and even greater when combined with high quality stiff-fibred hackles which actually hinder a successful hooking. Because I use many flies in the paradun style, (all my imitative flies and some of the fancy patterns such as the Sturdy's Fancy are tied in this way,) I believe the problem I face is not so great. The entire body of the paradun rests on or below the surface; it is generally deeper in the film than a small shoulder-hackled pattern and so it is less likely to be moved beyond reach by the small pressure force. Also the bend of the hook hangs lower in the water. Therefore, I believe that I have a noticeably higher hooking ratio with paraduns than with small conventional flies for grayling.

One incident comes to mind in support of the theory. A Canadian friend Paul Marriner and I were fishing the Waterdown river in Northern Saskatchewan. I had been using the Klinkhamer successfully but Paul had chosen one of the most popular North American dry flies, a size 16 Parachute Adams. In a little over an hour Paul caught twenty-eight grayling from a run about fifteen feet long. They were all excellent fish measuring between fifteen and nineteen inches. The most significant aspect is that he took them in no more than about forty casts. The Parachute Adams is a paradun with the body on or in the film. I have my doubts whether conventionally hackled flies would have deceived or hooked so many.

There is no need for despair if you miss rising grayling. They are not as wary as trout in this respect and having missed a fly will happily rise again before being really put down providing they have not been pricked on the strike. They are often very tolerant of repeated presentations. As with all grayling fly fishing, if after repeated casting over a shoal they go off a pattern, change to something else and they often react with a renewed appetite. Even if the shoal scatters after a bad cast, they usually reform not far away or return within a few minutes and start to feed again.

If rising grayling are proving difficult with the patterns and styles of dry fly you are showing them, try fishing with a finer leader point and changing fly size. Dropping down a size or two is likely best, but on occasion a larger pattern will succeed. Certainly when fishing for Scandinavian grayling the advice would be to try a bigger pattern.

I have benefited more than once from a tip passed on to me by an angler in his seventies with a lifetime of fishing behind him. His most effective dry-fly fishing aid was a pair of scissors with which he cut and trimmed to reshape hackles, wings, tails and bodies in search of the elusive shape that grayling and trout wanted. This doctoring produced a fly box of unrecognisable patterns; a scrap of Sturdy's Fancy, half a Hare's Ear, a bit of a Black Gnat, a wingless Wickham or a truncated Terry's Terror. He caught a lot of grayling and trout with this mutilated menagerie.

Until recently I was entirely convinced that both trout and grayling could be leader-shy, ie, from time to time their sight of the floating tippet deterred them rising. Lars-Åke Olsson has been trying to convince me that the leader-shy grayling (or trout) doesn't exist. In fact, he maintains that except on the most rippled surface, whether the tippet sinks or floats, fish are aware of it but do not know what to make of it. After all, fish rise readily to dry flies when the floating tippet is very obviously visible, why should they sometimes find it unacceptable? Drag has a much greater influence. Fish are critical of even the micro-drag created by too thick or too stiff a leader, and a softer or finer tippet may answer the problem. However, all aspects of presentation are very important and I am unconvinced that fish ignore sight of the tippet. Lars and other well respected and internationally known fly fishers prefer a floating leader and tippet because it is easier to strike on a fish and it doesn't pull under a small dry fly. Lars greases his leader to the fly and consequently, in many situations it must be very obvious to a fish. I certainly wouldn't want to compete head to head with Lars in a dry-fly fishing competition but for the time being I prefer my last eighteen inches of tippet to sink to avoid its more obvious presence on the surface.

If you think grayling are leader-shy, one of the most obvious ways of improving the presentation is to fish downstream. Now the fish sees the fly before the leader.There is nothing new in this. Roger Woolley[9] was possibly the first advocate of the downstream dry fly for grayling, aware of

[9] *The Grayling* by Richard Lake, second edition 1946 with chapters by Roger Woolley. Woolley's views were also recorded by W. Carter Platts in *Grayling Fishing* 1939

what he considered to be their critical eyesight and being leader-shy. Continental grayling fishers have long practised this approach and there it is as common as the upstream method. Perhaps we have been slower to adapt in Britain because of the traditional approach that dictated a dry fly should be fished upstream. Not only is the downstream cast effective when using small flies in slow, clear water but it has considerable advantages when trying to control the drift of a fly in a riffle. When casting across the stream in fast water the current pulls on the line and the fly. So, without mending the line, drag soon sets in and the cast is quickly fished out.

Longer drifts can be obtained by mending and reaching and by different casting and presentation techniques, like the parachute cast, that produce slack line and leader. When standing at the head of a pool or riffle it is possible to cast the fly with slack leader and line into the required feeding lane and by mending, reaching and even releasing more line achieve longer drifts than when fishing upstream. Sometimes it is easier to search out every possible feeding lane by controlling the fly from upstream. The consistently successful grayling angler is the master of all methods of presentation.

5

The Subsurface Fly

'In the swift places of the river the grayling rests, a fish of silver and pearl, fanning the stream gently with graceful fronds of bronze silk. He looks as if he rested still, and let the stream ripple though his soft fins, but he is keeping his pace with effortless grace. Sometimes he lets go and drifts down stream, swift as the shadow of a flying bird; and then a flicker of pearl light, and he is back at rest again. At evening time when the stream is dark, he shines like white pewter in the moonlight.'

Dorothy Hartley, *Food in England*

WITH MORE FISHERMEN prepared to start their grayling season half-way through the trout season, dry-fly fishing for grayling has become more popular. There is more surface food about during the summer months and grayling are willing risers. However, I have little doubt that in the traditional grayling season from October onwards the nymph or wet-fly fisher catches more fish. After all, grayling take the majority of their food from below the surface and there is a marked tendency for grayling to feed from the river bed as they grow older. Except during a period of surface feeding the logical way to fish is with a fly into their territory.

At the turn of the century the options for the grayling wet-fly fisher were few. His wet flies would sink a few inches below the surface unless he chose to use the infamous Grasshopper[1] of Francis Francis fame. This heavily leaded green wool lure was usually baited with maggots or worms so it is difficult to classify as a forerunner of our modern bugs. Fished on its own it might have passed for an obese *Rhyacophila* larva, but it seems to have been rarely used without an attached bait.

The first to write about incorporating lead in a proper fly specifically for grayling was H.A. Rolt, author of *Grayling Fishing in South Country Streams* (1901). This allowed more depth to be achieved and gave the angler greater scope. Until Rolt's idea spread, wet-fly fishers elsewhere were presenting their spider patterns and wet flies just below the surface. Still, nymph patterns remained largely unweighted for trout fishing, but for grayling, Dr E.A. Barton[2] in the 1930s or possibly earlier, was dressing nymph imitations with an underbody of a length of fuse wire laid along the shank. Frank Sawyer writes[3] of observing Brig. General H.E. Carey catching grayling on a nymph in 1928 and subsequently watching him catch big grayling on nymphs fished deep. Some of these were weighted and were no doubt sowing seeds of an idea that later produced the weighted Pheasant Tail nymph and the Killer Bug. Sawyer acknowledged that Carey 'showed me how to make nymphs and that grayling could be deceived with them.' But perhaps the forerunner of the Pheasant Tail nymph goes back even further. The French fly fisherman, Jean Lysik, devised his heavily weighted nymph[4] in 1873 and it is in many ways very similar to Sawyer's creation. For interest I will give the dressing: the abdomen and pronounced thorax are made by winding medium copper wire enamelled purple. The tails are pheasant tail fibres, the abdomen is covered with wound peacock or heron herl and the wingcase over the

[1] Francis's Grasshopper illustrations (1867) were taken from an earlier book, Hewett Wheatley's *The Rod and the Line* (1849). Wheatley devised a leaded Mayfly nymph to be fished on the bottom in the sink and draw style. The book's subtitle was *Or practical hints and dainty devices, for the sure taking of trout, grayling, etc.* My attention is drawn to the reference in the title to grayling. Perhaps here is the first ever weighted grayling bug

[2] Recorded by W. Carter Platts in *Grayling Fishing*, 1939

[3] *Nymphs and the Trout* by Frank Sawyer. First edition (1958) refers to 1927, later editions mention the year as 1928, presumably correcting the first edition

[4] The Nymphe Jeannot is described in *French Fishing Flies* by Jean-Paul Pequegnot (1984) English language edition 1987

exposed thorax of wire is pheasant or heron fibres. There are strong parallels between the two designs but I cannot say if Sawyer was influenced by the earlier French nymph. There may have been other European developments for achieving depth for grayling of which I am unaware, but so far as the British fly fisher was concerned, all we had (and it seemed, all we needed) were a few moderately leaded wet flies, the Pheasant Tail nymph, and Sawyer's Grayling or Killer Bug. This latter dramatically altered chalk stream fishing for grayling and had some influence on other rivers. For the first time an artificial could be presented on the bottom with a fly rod and fished in the conventional style of the upstream nymph. If a heavy enough bug was used, a depth of six or seven feet in slow water could be achieved. As far as I am aware, Sawyer never gave a specific year in which he developed either the Killer Bug or his famous nymph but they both belong to the period before the Second World War. It was not until Sawyer published *Keeper of the Stream* in 1952 and *Nymphs and the Trout* in 1958 that they gained wider currency.

Prior to the Killer Bug, fly fishermen on rainfed rivers were barely scraping the surface with a team of wet flies. When grayling are in the runs and glides and are prepared to rise to a fly higher in the water these methods will succeed but grayling often feed close to the bottom, where no normal wet fly or spider pattern is ever fished. This is one reason why trotting, i.e., float fishing with worms or maggots, was necessary if grayling were to be caught during autumn and winter days when they refused to feed away from the river bed. Bait fishing will always be extremely effective because it enables the bait to be presented accurately at depth. However, in recent years there have been some developments in fly fishing techniques, tackle and fly design that have revolutionised bottom level fly fishing in rivers. The grayling fisher has been the main beneficiary. It won't mean an end to trotting for grayling because during adverse water conditions bait fishing remains more efficient. It does mean though that the fly fisherman now has more options.

One of the most useful aids for subsurface fly fishing is a pair of polarising sunglasses. Except on the dullest days, I always wear a pair for all my fishing. They reveal much more of the subsurface world by reducing the surface glare. Consequently, they allow more fish movements to be seen than without them. When nymph and wet-fly fishing they can mean many more fish being caught, and when trying to spot fish in waters they are invaluable.

BUG FISHING

The bug patterns we use are not nymphs in the conventional sense, i.e., they do not represent any natural nymph, but the manner of presenting them upstream on a floating line is very similar. The original Grayling or Killer Bug was to my knowledge, for many years the only heavily weighted bug for grayling until the ever-inventive Richard Walker produced the Mead Mill Special[5], devised probably in the early 1970s. A few other heavy shrimp patterns began to show up and in an effort to find my own answer I experimented with a heavily weighted seal's fur bug. I varied the colours considerably and found that all natural colours worked equally. Even by today's bug standards my Dove Bug was an extremely simplistic answer to the problem, but it worked well. For too long I had used just the Killer Bug, but with a second choice I now had an alternative to offer when a shoal became wary of seeing the same fly. I wrote in *The Grayling Angler* that bug fishing was still in its infancy and predicted that this method would develop as an answer to the problem of deep-lying grayling. I would like to think my foresight was correct, except that my crystal ball didn't foresee those of a different hue or the wide range of modern bug and caddis larva patterns which have opened up so many new opportunities for grayling fishing.

Central European fly fishers had been using glass and metal beads around the turn of the century, but their flies apparently attracted little attention. When Roman Moser introduced us to his gold-headed bugs for Austria's River Traun in the 1980s, I thought with some certainty that here was a truly new and highly successful development. I was wrong on the first count, but right on the second. No other fly-tying development has so radically altered the way we fish for deep-lying grayling and trout.

Prominent in the pantheon of grayling flies are gold, copper, silver or black bead-headed nymphs and bugs. So successful are these patterns on some rivers that it could be so easy to use them to the exclusion of all

[5] The pattern is probably now defunct. For those interested in the dressing it was: Hook size 10-16 with 3 layers of lead foil bound on the back with olive thread. The body was three parts grass-green wool well mixed with one part lime-green fluorescent wool and ribbed with fine gold thread. The back was speckled turkey tail feather fibres with 2 fibres of the same for legs extending as far back as the rear of the body. From *Dick Walker's Modern Fly Dressings* (1980)

other fly types. The same is true of the Killer Bug, which can be so effective on several rivers that from October until February it is all that is required. The fly fisher may give no further thought to fly selection, grayling behaviour or entomology; a single bug may catch a good number of grayling on every fishing trip. It is possible to fish in such a way on some streams but who wants to? The monotony of fishing style and pattern selection would soon become too tedious and repetitive to hold much interest. Much of fly-fishing's fascination is the challenge of selecting a successful combination of fly pattern and presentation. A Killer Bug, or just one type of bead-head fly, may enable you to catch very many grayling throughout the season, but far more will be caught by adapting to their feeding habits.

There was a period in the 1980s when I enjoyed grayling fishing of a very high standard as a guest of Stephen Madden, a member of the Driffield Angler's Club. The club controls a pleasant few miles of a Yorkshire chalk stream. When writing *The Grayling Angler* I wrote to the club, chancing my arm and slightly tongue in cheek, explaining that although I was preparing a book on grayling, my chalk stream experience was minimal and to broaden my education could I be permitted a day's fishing after the trout season had ended? To their credit and my continued gratitude both Stephen Madden and the keeper, Tony Waites, permitted me unrestricted access for grayling after the end of September from that first year until the early 1990s. I visited on average three times each October and November in search of the elusive three pounder but I never landed one over two pounds six ounces. Tony Waites' reports of large grayling seen when netting the beck spurred me on. Incidentally, grayling from the Driffield West Beck have possibly the fastest growth rates in the country.

I did a little dry-fly fishing for grayling on the Driffield Beck but mainly all that was required was a Killer Bug. The dead drift worked well enough. Occasionally they wanted it with a little upward or sideways movement. That one pattern, fished throughout the autumn and winter, caught hundreds of grayling. I would ring the changes with a Dove Bug when a shoal wearied of the Killer Bug. However, it would have been as easy to move to the next shoal, resting the first for twenty minutes or so before returning. The clear water permitted a good view of the shoals and grayling behaviour. Unfortunately, as the water levels dropped from year to year, grayling became more tightly packed in the pools until the fishing lost its appeal. Sometimes the bigger grayling, instead of fighting deep, would fight at the top, making long runs close to the surface with the red-tinged dorsal fin breaking through like a shark's and shining brightly in all its colours in the autumn sun. Those big fish were perfectly marked and were wonderful specimen grayling. I doubt if I will enjoy grayling fishing of that quality again. I never bettered the three grayling for six pounds one ounce which came in a memorable ten minutes' fishing.

Frank Sawyer originally tied the Killer Bug as a shrimp imitation. It certainly is, but he later thought that it could also represent the pupa of the brown silverhorn sedge and a beetle larva. Some other bug patterns are clearly also shrimp imitations, but what of the more gaudily dressed bead-head bugs so much in recent favour? The only reason grayling take any artificial is that it passes for natural food. Occasionally grayling may mouth some passing debris with the intention of testing it for edibility. Grayling take gold heads, et al, readily, believing them to be food. If the fish were merely curious as to what the passing gold head might be, these patterns would be nowhere near as successful as they are.

Nondescript bugs, shrimps, caddis larvae, pupae and true nymph patterns can all be tied in the bead-head style. Sometimes the colour and brightness of the bead-head are significant. On the credit side, the shiny reflective metal draws attention to the fly in murky water where visibility is poor, but to its detriment, in clear, sunny conditions the metal bead can be so bright as to make fish wary. I now rarely use gold-coloured beads because they can appear unnaturally bright. On sunny days I have watched small groups of grayling actually move away, without even a cursory interest as a gold head moved through the shoal. I prefer the more subdued copper, which appears just as effective as gold in murky water and is much more acceptable in clear.

For the last couple of years I have been experimenting with black metal beads made of tungsten. They cost twice as much, but are twice as heavy, as other metal beads and so are an attractive way of gaining additional weight without additional bulk. The result is that small flies will sink deeper. I have caught many grayling and trout on these darker bead patterns. Sometimes when the brighter bead patterns have exhausted a grayling shoal I use the black metal beads to take fish, and they definitely have an advantage in bright sun to wary fish, but as a first line approach to a grayling I tend to stay with copper-coloured beads. I have found the black tungsten versions very effective for trout on one particularly clear stream. Often trout in this water shy away from bugs incorporating shiny beads but they don't seem to notice the black ones. The simplest creation of all is extremely effective. A shaggy hare's fur body on a long shank 14 or 16 hook with the black tungsten bead-head is a very acceptable cased caddis imitation.

The high visibility of the reflective bead is also important for the angler. When casting to visible grayling it is a great advantage to be able to see the artificial as it drifts towards an individual fish or approaches a shoal. More naturally coloured bugs and nymphs are camouflaged against the background of the river bed, but the reflective bead often allows the fly to be tracked accurately. This allows any movement induced by the angler to be given at the right time and, importantly, the grayling's reaction to the fly is more closely monitored.

As to whether the bead itself represents any aspect of the natural insect is debatable. It has been suggested that on caddis pupa imitations the ball is mistaken for an air bubble or part of the translucent sheath that is sometimes seen on the natural. It seems feasible, but as black bead patterns also work well the flash of the bead seems to be at most a weak trigger.

Beads also help to achieve considerable depth. Bead-head flies may be weighted in two ways. The first is with just the weight of the bead, and the second is with additional lead foil or wire or copper wire under the body. It is not an exaggeration to say that a tungsten bead pattern with a lead underbody will sink as fast as a stone. The rapid attainment of depth is essential when attempting to present a bug to grayling lying in deep pools or at the heads of fast runs. Normal patterns either fail to reach the fish, or in fast water they don't get down fast enough to cover fish at the upper limit of the lie. I can think of a number pools that shelve off rapidly and have a near vertical drop of two or three feet or more at the head of the pool. It is in such pools that bigger grayling take up residence, or perhaps it is simply that because an angler's normal flies cannot be presented on the bottom there that the grayling survive to grow large.

The final feature of a bead-head pattern that carries no additional underbody weighting is that the heaviest will fish head-down. When they are moved by the fly-fisher the head will rise first, and sink first. This change of pitch can be repeated. It is a more exaggerated movement than a nymph or bug weighted only under the body.

Perhaps the strangest and most unlikely bead nymphs are the Piam series from the French fly fisherman after whom they are named. I first saw these in 1994 and half dismissed them as some Gallic aberration, as quirky as the Citroen 2CV, as subtly coloured as the Pompidou Centre, and of no relevance to the grayling I fish for. It seems I underestimated them. These small nymphs have a gold or black bead-head and a short tapered pre-formed lead body which is painted, usually a single colour. For many, that is the complete 'dressing' although a few may be ribbed or have a short tail. All are extremely small. A size 16 hook is large, sizes 18 or 20 standard and even a size 22 is not unknown. I have seen them in post-box red, day-glow orange, vivid green and bright yellow but some sombre colours are also used. They are fished on the clear French limestone and chalk streams to visible grayling. They sink extremely quickly and can be manipulated in front of the fish. As can be imagined, the nymphs themselves are relatively easy to see. I was reintroduced to these in 1998, and through the kindness of Vincent Piriou, the secretary of the French branch of the Grayling Society, I found myself using some on our English grayling, which showed signs of being as gullible as their Gallic cousins. In my limited use of the Piam nymphs they were moderately successful. I have not had the opportunity to experiment fully, but I would imagine that grayling which have become accustomed to the larger bugs and are more wary, might be less cautious over these tiny bugs. I enjoy fishing small flies and here is one series of small nymphs that sink very quickly and yet can be fished with a very fine presentation.

So successful are bugs on some rivers that if anglers killed all the fish they caught they could decimate grayling stocks in a short period. Sawyer's intention in creating the Killer Bug was to have a means of controlling the grayling stocks on the Avon, and you can only achieve that with a fly pattern if it is outstandingly reliable over many months of the season. If one rod can catch over a hundred grayling a day, and I have seen this happen quite a few times with the use of various bugs, the method may be more effective than netting. On a handful of occasions I have caught between a hundred and a hundred and fifty grayling in an October day on a southern chalk stream. Sometimes half the catch has been on dry fly but mostly they have been on nymphs, or more accurately, on bugs, but I wouldn't want to repeat the feat every time I went grayling fishing. Like most anglers, I would prefer to work a little harder and believe that my fewer fish were the result of a thoughtful, reasoned application of skill against a wily and elusive species.

Bug fishing for grayling developed on the chalk streams but it has been adopted on all other grayling rivers and works very well. The method is very simple. The weighted bug is cast well upstream of the grayling lie. In some clear rivers it will be possible to see the grayling, perhaps just an individual or more likely, a shoal, but on many rainfed rivers it will be a matter of fishing blind into the likely lies. The bug should be fished on the same level as the grayling, ie, close to the stream bed. This is invariably done with a floating line (I use no other on a river) and an appropriately long leader – mine are usually about twelve feet. If you are fortunate to fish for visible grayling, their reaction to the bug may be quite clear. Being able to track the bug is a bonus as usually the fly will not be seen. If the fly is visible, the takes will be obvious. It can be lifted and the fish induced to take through the bug's movement as it bears down on the fish. When fishing to unseen fish, the takes will register through the movement of the line or leader, or by movement of the bite indicator now so commonly used. In a weedy river or over an uneven river bed, the drift of a heavy bug will be interrupted quite often and this will register as a take. Any indication of a take must be reacted to, whether a pause in the downstream drift or a more positive movement.

I am fortunate to fish a number of streams for visible grayling; sometimes these may be no more than one or two fish, but others are shoals of thirty, fifty, seventy or more. They can be carefully approached from behind and if I remain still for some minutes they may drop downstream to within a few feet of me. Some of these rivers are clear chalk streams but others are rainfed streams and rivers, which at summer levels reveal far more of their inhabitants than in autumn and winter. The intimacy of grayling fishing on small clear streams is challenging and rewarding. When fishing for visible grayling I have learned a lot about what they think of my different nymphs, bugs and dry flies. I also find this to be possibly the most satisfying and exciting way of catching grayling, when I can see them clearly and I can monitor their every reaction. It is certainly a lot of fun.

One thing that soon becomes clear, and it is equally true when dry-fly fishing, is that grayling may ignore the fly completely as it passes, then turn downstream to follow and take it. Sometimes it can be the induced movement of the nymph or bug that provokes the late interest, at other times it is merely as though the fish has had second thoughts about letting food pass by.

Most grayling are remarkably tolerant of a careful wading angler. Even in clear unrippled water of a foot or so depth it is quite possible to end up casting to a shoal just ten feet away. Sometimes they become wary of the bug continuously passing through, the encroaching human legs or the repeated commotion of one of their relatives mysteriously gyrating about and disappearing. Sometimes the shoal will gradually move upstream, merging with other pockets of fish until unwilling to move further and you end up fishing to an extraordinary number of fish. Some will drop back downstream to the original position and continue to feed unaffected by the disruption. I have noticed that when wanting to keep the shoal in the same place, it is better to ease up fishing for five minutes and let the grayling settle back to their original position.

Away from the chalk streams, at higher water than low summer levels, most fishing will be to unseen grayling. If the angler is behind the fish, grayling will make some upstream progression. If the takes ease up, it may be because the fish have moved upstream. Simply because they cannot be seen by the angler doesn't mean that they behave differently to sighted fish, although the angler has more chance of remaining undetected. Monitoring their takes to the nymph or bug can be quite a challenge. Sometimes grayling take very confidently and movement of the line or leader is obvious, especially in a fairly swift flow. But at other times grayling will take a fly and reject it so quickly that there is no indication on the line or leader. These fish are well nigh impossible to catch unless they can actually be seen. Fishing blind, you may never be aware of any grayling interest and pass them by, frustrated at failing to find fish. Sometimes the sign of the take is slight and this too is hard to detect. If the fishing area is distant and the surface rippled or the light difficult, spotting the takes is impractical if all one is watching is the floating leader.

For this reason, in the late 1970s I started to tie on my leader a short length of knitting wool soaked in floatant to act as a bite indicator when winter grayling fishing. I don't remember where I had the idea from but it wasn't original, although few anglers used it. In difficult conditions it improved my catch rate by a few hundred percent. Indicators have become more sophisticated today and are quite commonplace when nymph fishing for trout and grayling. They are even being used on stillwaters.

From time to time, in appropriate circumstances, I use an indicator, but it remains a piece of coloured poly yarn. Usually my appropriate circumstances are when I am unable to see the floating leader butt, and I generally restrict its use to when a bug pattern is being fished deep at a distance, or when detection, for other reasons is more difficult. For all other subsurface fishing I usually rely on more conventional methods of detection. The indicator fulfils the role a float plays for the bait fisher. It allows a bug to be presented at a very accurate depth, on any number of successive casts, and therefore permits a degree of repetition with precision which is unprecedented with more traditional fly fishing methods. My attitude towards indicators hasn't changed over the years. I believe that their over-use produces lazy fishermen because they minimise the skills required for line and leader observation. I do not mean to sound intolerant or unsympathetic towards a novice. Use them if you find them necessary to catch fish. My advice is that indicators should be used only when necessary, and that those occasions will reduce as experience is gained.

When cast upstream, the bug or heavy nymph will sink to its required depth and continue to drift downstream. The dead drift works well but sometimes it might be necessary or helpful to lift the bug or move it one side to simulate the movement of a natural insect. Whenever the cast is fished out, whether still upstream, opposite or slightly downstream of the angler, lift the rod and line as the first part of the action in recasting. This will cause the artificial to rise in the water and is often the point at which a grayling reacts. It is easy to miss these takes in the initial stages of recasting because they are unexpected. Concentrate on the line end or leader where it enters the water and include the lifting process at the end of each drift as part of the fishing technique and more grayling will be caught.

On a stream with a relatively smooth river bed the current will be of a fairly constant moderate pace. On most streams there is a much more uneven flow over rocks, stones, sand, through riffles, glides, fast shallows and slow, deep pools. There will be a wider range of current speeds. It is worth remembering that on the stream bed the current is slower than at the surface, very often less than half the surface speed and that grayling can find very much quieter lies on the river bed in pockets and depressions when the surface current is passing above them at a considerable pace. A heavy bug that sinks through the current can be fished to these grayling. The only problem is that as the fly line is taken up at the speed of the surface current, there is not much time for the bug to be fished at the speed of the current at the bottom. One answer is to fish at a short distance and to keep the fly line off the surface and Eastern European grayling anglers have become expert at this. The Tuck Cast is an excellent means of getting weighted nymphs to sink as quickly as possible.

THE LEADHEAD NYMPH

When I invited Hans van Klinken in 1988 to fish the Dove, a small tributary of the River Rye in North Yorkshire, he brought with him the Leadhead, a pattern I had first fished successfully earlier that year on the River Kyll in Germany. I had caught trout and grayling with it on the Kyll but I didn't try it again until Hans fished with me in October. To be quite honest, I didn't like the look of the fly, a shaggy bug well over an inch long with a lead split shot attached at the head; it seemed out of place on a stream not much more than a beck, where small dry flies worked quite well and where my Dove Bug, at less than half its size, seemed to be the biggest bug anybody had thought of using. Just as he had on the Kyll, Hans proceeded to take grayling (and a few trout) from areas of the river I had never fished, believing them too fast, too turbulent or too shallow to justify any attention. My diary recalls that I caught eight grayling on the Dove Bug and Hans had between twenty and twenty-five, mainly on the Leadhead. Two days later, one of the wildest and windiest days I have fished on, we joined Roy Shaw on the Driffield Beck around Bell Mills. Hans caught among many others, a 47 cm grayling, the biggest of his trip, again on the Leadhead.

Like many of Hans' patterns, the Leadhead was devised for Scandinavian grayling; this one for fish in deep, almost unreachable lies. Something heavy but foodlike needed to be offered. One of the main items in grayling diets is the cased caddis, especially Scandinavian grayling where the caddis population is probably even denser than on our rivers. When fished in a dead drift close to the bottom, the Leadhead is a very good imitation of a large cased caddis. It needs no explanation or justification of its use. It has gone on to inspire other cased caddis patterns utilising the split shot weight at the head of the fly.

When fished on a floating line cast upstream and allowed to drift drag-free bouncing just above the bottom it catches a lot of grayling. Because it fishes head down and point upwards snagging the bottom is minimised but not eliminated. Because the Leadhead sinks quickly and continues to sink to the bottom, detecting takes is not easy because there are so many false knocks from the fly bouncing along the stream bed. This is one pattern when I am trying to achieve a dead drift on the bottom for which I will use a bite indicator, because the indicator acts as a float and suspends the fly at a constant depth. As the fly comes downstream, mend the line upstream or use a reach cast to allow as long a dead drift as possible. Hans will sometimes lift the fly as it continues its course. Certainly at the end of the drift, control the line so that the current picks up the leader and nymph and causes it to lift. Depending on the current speed, it will not be the dramatic swinging rise to the surface that occurs with lighter nymphs but it will lift a foot or two and be the stimulus for some grayling to take it. This method can be fished in all current speeds and depths because the nymph sinks so quickly. It is also possible to take grayling only six or eight feet away by careful wading. If the fishing area is only a rod's length away directly across the current, the nymph is cast upstream and the fly line may be lifted clear of the water as it drifts into the target zone.

The key to fishing any fly is not so much the pattern itself but how it is fished; otherwise the best fly tiers or those who could afford the best-tied flies would catch all the fish. The Leadhead is a highly ambiguous pattern with a Jekyll and Hyde character. In a dead-drift it is a cased caddis, but start to move the fly across the current or upstream it changes its role completely. As soon as it starts to move away from a dead-drift it becomes, to my mind, a bullhead, minnow or other small fish. It has the shape and general colouring of a fish, even a mobile tail to imitate the fast wiggle of the natural and a weighted head to ensure the head-down attitude of a fish foraging, darting about the bottom. And it as a small fish imitation that it continues to catch grayling and trout.

Grayling take small fish, although they do not feature highly in autopsies. I have caught them when pike spinning and on streamers like a Micky Finn in Scandinavia. Other anglers tell of big grayling caught on salmon flies. When the Leadhead is moved across the current or upstream I am sure its success with grayling can only be because it imitates a small fish. It is often only the larger fish that respond to this style. When I saw Hans first fish the Leadhead on the Kyll and the Dove he retrieved it upstream through fast, shallow riffles which at the time I doubted would hold grayling. As so often when fishing with Hans, I was proved wrong.

CASELESS CADDIS

Twenty years ago, fishing a caseless caddis was almost unheard of in the U.K. In North America a few anglers had realised their value for trout in a riffle, but elsewhere we remained in our blissful state. Their importance to grayling on most rivers should not be underestimated. Although they may not feature as a major food source in surveys of stomach contents they are avidly taken by grayling and trout. The caseless caddis larvae are in a minority compared to cased larvae, but they are consumed at a higher ratio than their numbers suggest, ie, grayling express a preference for them over the cased caddis.

As adult fly life reduces as autumn progresses, grayling look to take more of their food from the river bed, and as all insect activity on the bottom is scarcer, grayling begin to grub about for food. The larvae of some free-swimming caddis species are mature or close to maturity throughout the winter and their imitation is becoming one of the surest ways of catching autumn and winter grayling lying deep on the bottom. I have caught my share of grayling in such a way but the testimony of two friends, both very experienced grayling fishers, speaks for itself. Bernard Benson caught a twenty inch (fifty one centimetre) grayling on a caseless caddis from a pool on the Ure I fish regularly. I am ever hopeful of a recapture. Lars-Åke Olsson recalls two three pounders in successive casts on a green caddis larva.

One of the methods of presentation is with the Eastern European short nymph style mentioned in the following section. Alternatively, the imitation can be fished more conventionally singly or with a second imitation on a dropper on a short leader and a floating line. It also works well in only moderately-paced water to thigh depth as a point fly on a three fly leader fished upstream and across. The essential element to its success is to present it close to the bottom.

When fishing either the *Rhyacophila* or *Hydropsyche* imitation as a single fly on a floating leader, there is some value in using a weighted braided leader if there is fast water or fast and deep pools.The Roman Moser types with a centre core of a metal insert are very effective and the most pleasing to use. A short level mono leader of about three feet and approximately four pounds breaking strain is adequate. Make the cast almost diagonally upstream and mend the line as it drifts, or extend the drift in any way by reaching. Many of the takes come at the point when the imitation begins to lift off the bottom. Always present it with short casts. Keep in close touch with the fly by keeping as little of the line as possible on the surface and thoroughly work through likely holding water. The takes will register as firm tugs, a pause in the drift, or line movement.

POLISH AND CZECH NYMPH TECHNIQUES

Just a few years ago, in the UK we were hearing of a mysterious fly fishing style known as the Czech Nymph method, which it was rumoured had achieved prodigious catches of grayling and trout. Perhaps I have exaggerated slightly, as all new foreign techniques seem to be veiled by an air of mystery which promise more and bigger grayling by secret and esoteric fishing styles. I am grateful to my friend Jurek Kowalski, captain of the Polish fly fishing team and President of FIPS-Mouche[6] for explaining both the history of the technique and the fishing method.

This technique first developed in the late 1970s for grayling fishing on the Polish River Dunajec by anglers from this mountainous area, and in 1981 the Polish national championship was won using this style. The Polish team adopted the technique wherever grayling and trout were to be found in deep, fast water. In 1985 they won the team and individual world title on the Polish River San, a feat they repeated in 1989 in Finland, and the following year on the Welsh Dee they had the individual winner and were second to the Czechs in the team competition. The method is now proving extremely successful on rivers all over the world. For a brief time the technique was misnamed as the 'rolling nymph' and at the moment, much to Polish consternation, it is commonly referred to as 'Czech nymphing'. The Poles call it the 'short nymph' because of the small length of line beyond the rod tip. The method is still developing and varies slightly in a number of ways. I will describe the general principle but there are variations on the number of flies fished, the distance

[6] International Federation of Sports Fly Fishing

between the droppers, the amount of fly line beyond the rod tip, the length of the fishing zone and the movement of the flies.

Grayling in deep fast water had remained fairly secure from fly fishermen who generally believed that no fly could penetrate the current to be presented on the bottom. I and others have used variations on the American, Charles Brooks' method with a sinking line, or with a floating line and weighted braided leaders, for fishing deep in these lies, with modest success. When a more effective and easier method of presentation was devised it was inevitable that it would catch a lot of fish; mainly grayling that hitherto had either never seen an artificial or had never seen one of this type, presented in these circumstances. Wherever it is introduced the method is capable of catching grayling and trout from previously unfished lies. Older grayling have a bias towards bottom feeding, and as the Woolland survey showed in Chapter Two, they also have a preference for cased and free-swimming, caseless, caddis larvae, the very patterns the Polish method employs. No wonder it has established a formidable reputation and become much copied by other national teams who have taken it back to their own countries. Unfortunately, Jurek Kowalski now fishes the style much less, even though he fishes on suitable rivers. His concerns about using the style too frequently are caused by the effectiveness of the method and the consequences of this, ie, overfishing, and the narrowing of the fisherman's skills because of the tendency to restrict oneself to a single method.

On the River Dunajec and others in the area, grayling were abundant until the mid 1980s and catches of sixty or seventy were possible. The deep, short nymph technique was developed by experienced grayling fly fishermen looking for new methods and applied their knowledge of grayling lies, habits and food sources with the invention of the new technique. The new and effective technique developed at a time when there was a significant increase in fly fishing in Poland. As a result, many Polish rivers became overfished and the quality of the fishing dropped considerably, although it has now fully recovered. After all the easier grayling had been caught, anglers went on to hunt out the more difficult fish in the faster depths. Even this last refuge proved assailable by those anglers with the intent, ingenuity and ignorance to pursue the elusive survivors. Jurek describes it as 'the method to catch the last grayling in the river.' There is a salutory lesson in this for all fly fishermen. I have no doubt that we are more efficient anglers than a generation ago; our methods and tackle allow us to make effective presentations to fish we could not reach twenty years ago. I do not find the methods themselves inherently wrong, but the indiscriminate killing of fish and the misuse of any method should be strictly guarded against. Responsible river management and angler education should ensure that grayling survive and thrive in a river. It was neither the intent to fish deep, fast water, nor the ingenuity to devise a method, that killed so many Polish grayling; it was ignorance. But for a brown trout restocking policy on a regular and frequent basis, many of our British, certainly English rivers would be devoid of trout through overfishing, or specifically, overkilling. The same must not be allowed to happen to grayling, the last truly wild game fish on many of our rivers.

The short nymph method usually employs two or three flies on the leader, but at low summer levels only a single fly may be possible. The intention is to achieve depth quickly so all the flies are weighted, with the heaviest usually going on the top dropper to ensure that the lighter ones are pulled to the bottom. Cased and free-swimming caddis larvae are the usual patterns because the naturals abound in fast water. Other bead-head patterns will work but where a natural imitation is acceptable I prefer to fish with one. Woven nymphs based on Eastern European patterns are gaining popularity but I have not found that they are more attractive to grayling; to fishermen certainly, but not to fish, and I don't have time to spare on tying more complex patterns when simple dressings work well. The patterns themselves are not very important and a wide range will prove acceptable. Some suitable ones are suggested in the final chapter. Seeing anything food-like in fast water grayling have to make their minds up quickly; there is no time for an examination of the finer points of imitation. In fact, what Jurek and his team colleague Adam Sikora[7], twice the runner-up in the individual World Championship, emphasize, is that the control of the flies is far more important than their colour, size, shape and construction. The main consideration for dressing is that they should sink quickly.

The leader is not tapered but level and should be as fine as the size and weight of the nymphs will permit. Snagging the bottom is common and potential losses must also be balanced. If you are not aware of the nymphs tapping the bottom when fishing you will not be fishing deep enough. The length of the leader from fly line to the top dropper should

[7] See Adam Sikora's chapter in *The World's Best Trout Flies* (1994) edited by the author

be one or two feet longer than the depth of the water. The distance between the flies may be as little as ten to twelve inches (25–30 cm) up to three or even five feet. In the fastest and deepest water the weight needs to be concentrated to get deep to the fish. However, in shallower, slower water, more bottom can be explored with flies further apart.

The distance between the angler and the fishing zone will never be much more than a rod's length. Grayling are remarkably tolerant of fishermen and by careful wading they can be approached to within a yard or so in the riffles and faster channels to be fished. The intention is to achieve a short dead drift close to the bottom. Takes are most obvious when there is the shortest possible distance from the rod tip to the flies. Standing approximately opposite the fishing zone, the angler casts or flicks his flies upstream and permits some fly line to rest on the surface to allow the flies to sink rapidly. When the flies have sunk and reached the fishing zone, then the rod tip is lifted so the line is off the surface so there is a direct line of contact from the rod tip to the flies without any fly line on the surface. The rod should follow them downstream keeping as close a contact as possible with the flies; this aspect is extremely important. The flies should maintain a dead drift without any sideways deviation. It is desirable, where possible, to hold back the flies slightly because the current speed at the bottom is slower than at the surface. The effective length of the bottom covered is rarely more than one and a half metres. The takes are monitored by watching the end of the fly line or the attached mono just above the surface as it hangs from the rod tip.The cast may be fished out with a firm strike of about a foot to make the nymphs rise. The majority of the takes come at this final stage. After the strike, allow the current to lift the nymphs and both grayling and trout will take as the nymphs rise. These takes are usually more obvious and will be felt through the line.

A common variation on this developing technique is to lead the flies through the lie so that they travel slightly faster than the current. Takes are felt more firmly.

The riffles and channels have to be thoroughly searched with this method because the natural drift is only in a narrow current lane. The water should be comprehensively fished out, progressing either upstream, or downstream and across a broad riffle, with frequent short casts. It is possible to wade very close to grayling and to approach brown trout quite close from downstream in rough water. Various depths can be fished depending upon the weight of the flies and the current. I find that the technique excels in fast water of up to two and a half to three feet deep where the penetration of nymphs is almost impossible by any other method but where close wading is possible. It is still effective in water twice this depth if the nymphs can get to the bottom quickly and it can be reached a rod's length away. Needless to say, the deep wading, constant recasting and leading the flies can be a very tiring way of fishing.

I am aware of pools on every rainfed river I fish that are unfishable in terms of getting a fly close to the bottom in a dead drift except through the short nymph method. May I sound a note of caution: such is our expertise and efficiency nowadays in catching more trout and grayling from all areas of the river that we need to give more consideration to our resources of wild fish of both species and how we treat them. We must ensure that mature breeding fish continue to thrive in our rivers. We need to be aware that with our improved fishing efficiency there is the requirement for greater responsibility towards the fish. I would like to think that on all the rivers I fish there are areas of the river that remain unfishable so that wild fish will always have some refuge from the intrusion of the angler. No sportsman wants to dominate his prey to the degree that there is no sanctuary. Perhaps, at the moment, the only area of the river that offers security for grayling is in the deep slow water that is less attractive to fly fishing methods, and long may it remain so.

TRADITIONAL NYMPHING

The usual style of nymphing for grayling, ie, with patterns representing true nymphs, permits weighted nymphs like the Pheasant Tail nymph to sink to a depth of only about two or three feet in slow water, or exceptionally, a little deeper. In faster water the depth they reach is even less. In the last few years heavier patterns have been created but even the heavier patterns like Oliver Edwards' Heptagenid Nymph are successful only with those fish in water of up to thigh depth and of only a moderate pace. In faster water their effective depth will be less.

Grayling take nymphs close to the bottom or those hanging from the meniscus on the point of emergence. They don't often take them mid-water. The exception is when grayling find nymphs more frequently mid-water but this is likely to be only on weedy chalk streams where free swimming nymph activity in, around and between the weed beds is common.

On most rainfed rivers where grayling are found there is a wide range of fly species and consequently of nymph types. The agile-darting and moss-creeping species dominate the chalk streams but elsewhere on stony rivers the flat stone-clingers are prolific. Surprisingly, the more accurate imitation of the common Heptagenid and Ecdyonurus nymphs went largely ignored until recently. We made do with the same nymphs for their imitation as we did for the much smaller, slimmer agile darters; that is until Oliver Edwards gave considerable thought and extensive trials to patterns imitating the stone-clingers. From midsummer onwards when in sunny conditions and low water, grayling may take up positions towards the heads of riffles where there are few better subsurface patterns than Edwards' Heptagenid Nymph for winkling them out. These stony areas of fast water are exactly these nymphs' habitat and where grayling and trout expect them. I don't think that the natural nymph gets caught up in the drift very often but the imitation works very well. It should be fished upstream into the head of a shallow riffle or a pocket of likely water and the takes monitored in the usual way by watching the behaviour of the leader and line. The streamy water below a riffle or where there is a glide of a constant knee depth which grayling favour are also ideal for this pattern.

Sawyer's Pheasant Tail nymph remains as possibly the best agile-darting imitation, whether to sighted grayling or to those being fished for unseen in the likely lies. I first try out the dead drift, and if that fails, I lift it slightly, hoping that the upward movement of the nymph will convince the sceptical fish. From July to the end of the season on my small North Yorkshire stream we invariably experience quite low water levels. The Pheasant Tail nymph is the ideal pattern for the favoured grayling glides of a constant depth. Once it sinks to the required depth grayling usually greet it with an enthusiastic response. For faster penetration in deeper or quicker water I may use one of many variations I tie with a small copper or black tungsten bead-head instead of the usual thorax. They are just as effective and sink more quickly. Other imitations of agile-darting species also work well but unless grayling are taking emergers, they must incorporate weight, either as an underbody or as a metal bead.

Sometimes the takes to the drifting nymph in fast shallow water can be very fast indeed, especially if the grayling are no bigger than ten inches (25 cm). The line darts forward in a short stab that it is almost impossible to react to. When grayling behave like this I retrieve the nymph in a long pull, or a series of short pulls, faster than the current. Some grayling intercept it, but others follow and take it. All take more firmly and because I am already in close contact with the nymph being retrieved hooking the fish is much more likely.

One of the many reasons I love the intimacy of small stream fishing is that in low water conditions it can offer some of the most challenging fly fishing I have encountered. The problems of approach and concealment, presentation, and the need for a back cast more accurate than the demanding forward cast necessitate considerable thought even before the first cast is made. In the years before I had the visual excitement of fishing on a chalk stream for trout and grayling, I sought out the visible trout and grayling on my small stream in low water conditions. With the stealth of a Sioux brave I would manoeuvre into a position to see the fish and be able to cast. It taught me a lot about fish behaviour and significantly, I saw for myself the speed at which small grayling will take and reject a nymph, and do so without any indication on the floating leader. It emphasised how ineffective and inefficient our take detection can be when fishing to invisible grayling. With any presentation that involves slack line between the nymph and the floating leader, or on slow or moderately paced water grayling can react without us ever being aware of them.

If you have the chance to see the grayling you are fishing for the chances of success are much higher. Either or both the nymph and fish can be monitored and any additional movement is imparted at the critical time with the grayling reaction quite clear. Even then, the speed of smaller grayling may take you unawares. They are much faster than any trout. Sawyer believed that he found an answer to the problem. 'I think that grayling will discover the deceit much more quickly than trout, but after getting the first one and treating the nymph or lure (Killer Bug) with its slime, I have often killed up to thirty fish from the same pool and had little difficulty in hooking them.'[8] I have never treated a fly in such a way but I guess that any fly once lodged in a grayling's mouth may absorb some of the flavour and smell of the fish and may make a rejection less instantaneous. I sometimes wonder whether Sawyer's trick of rubbing on

[8] *Keeper of the Stream* (1952) by Frank Sawyer

the slime is a subtle step away from fly fishing and imitation and closer to bait fishing making the hook taste and smell acceptable?

Sawyer wrote of catching sixty three grayling in two and a half hours by using the method and suggested that he could have easily gone on to kill a hundred but declined to avoid the monotony[9]. It may have been monotonous only for Sawyer who had a lifetime's daily access to the river; the rest of us have a much higher boredom threshold. I suspect that parts of the Avon are just as prolific today and that such catches are within the capabilities of most fisherman with the will and powers of concentration to see it through. One friend, Roy Chase, in a feat of perseverance and prestidigitation, caught (and returned) one hundred and fifty-five in six hours on the Avon. A grayling every two minutes or so is spectacular fishing, requiring remarkable dedication to the task, and means a very high ratio of grayling hooked to those which take the fly. Happily, I can say that on the parts of the Avon I have been privileged to be a guest on, grayling are returned and not killed.

WET FLIES AND SPIDERS

Away from the chalk streams most subsurface fly fishing has been with spider patterns and specialist grayling patterns. On some rivers bugs may have taken over from the more traditional methods, but wherever grayling are found, at the appropriate time, they respond well to flies fished in the foot just below the surface. Swimming nymphs on the way to emergence, pupae, emergers, drowned duns and terrestrials will be found in the upper layers and grayling move from the river bed to intercept them. If grayling are lying in a few feet of water and there is no fly life in the upper layers, it is expecting too much to hope that they will move away from where food can be found, to nearer the surface. Sometimes they will be co-operative but we should not be surprised if they are not. When they are feeding in the upper layers some of the traditional grayling flies and imitative spiders cannot be improved on.

I know of no better wet-fly fisherman than Oliver Edwards; certainly I have never seen a more ruthless or more successful searcher of

[9] Ibid

every inch of likely water. His thoroughness and expertise in the presentation of the subsurface fly ensures that he catches a lot of grayling and trout. A great deal of thought goes into his pattern selection and fly design, but the key is in how and when they are fished. When subsurface fishing, most of Oliver's grayling are caught either on a weighted nymph or caddis larva in a dead drift, or with a traditional spider pattern within four inches of the surface. The choice is whether to fish close to the bottom or near the surface, because grayling in rainfed rivers rarely feed midwater.

When grayling are feeding in the upper layers, or are willing to rise there to take an artificial fly I invariably fish with an imitative pattern. I save the more obviously attractor grayling wet flies for slightly coloured water or for late autumn and winter fishing. When there is evidence of fly life about grayling will be feeding on natural insects and the logical response is to fish their imitation.

Probably the easiest but least successful method of wet-fly fishing is to cast at about forty-five degrees downstream and across the current. The flies have little time to sink, they begin to drag across the current almost immediately and thereby fail in most aspects of a desirable presentation. Such a style will catch grayling, but rarely very many. A lot of plucks will be felt through the line but the resistance of the rod and line and the speed of the flies arcing sideways as grayling attempt to intercept them invariably means that few of the fish tempted are actually hooked.

As with all fishing, the closest water should be fished first. By careful wading, gradually the more distant glides, stickles or branches of the current may be fished. Rather than fishing a longer line at a distance, where the takes are more difficult to detect and the intervening current interferes with the drift of the line, I suggest trying to fish as short a line as possible. This will necessitate careful wading and fishing the areas closest to the angler. If I needed reminding of how tolerant grayling can be, just the day prior to writing this when fishing the Ure in late June I had grayling (and trout) rising within my arm's reach of where I was wading.

I fish with wet flies in two similar ways. The first is by facing the fishing zone square on and casting across the current upstream. This allows a little time for the team of three flies to sink a few inches. I hold the rod high with as little as possible of the fly line on the surface, and if necessary, mending the line upstream to ensure a drag-free dead drift. Takes may be seen by the flash of the turning fish below the surface, a swirl in the water, or the movement of the line or leader as it hangs in an arc from the rod tip to the surface. You may or may not want to allow the flies to swing below you at the end of the cast. This may well catch a few fish but it may also make grayling downstream more wary. At the end of the drift there is value in pausing, allowing the line to pause momentarily and the flies will lift slightly in the current. Any presentation that enables flies to rise towards the surface, however slightly, will help in the imitation of a nymph or pupa, and grayling will often take just at the point of recasting. It seems to make no difference to me whether I work my way up or downstream with successive casts. The secret is to move with as little disturbance as possible, playing grayling quickly away from the fishing zone and thoroughly search all the possible holding areas before wading through them to access other branches of the current.

Occasionally, grayling like the flies to be moved slightly, deviating from the natural drift. This is achieved by raising the rod and moving the line slightly as the drift continues. The additional movement seems to allay their suspicions.

The second type of presentation I make is more upstream than across. It may even be directly upstream, but just as likely it will be at angle between directly upstream and forty-five degrees across. For the same reasons a short line presentation is preferable to a longer one. By a careful approach one can fish for grayling less than a rod's length away, but again the fish closest should be covered first before looking to wade further or extend the distance cast. The benefits of this presentation are that by approaching in the grayling's blind spot directly behind the fish the angler has more chance of remaining undetected. Secondly, I find take detection easier with the movement of the line or leader more positive, and third, any raising of the rod will cause the flies to lift more directly towards the surface and not sideways across the current. This movement is more natural. Never more so than when fishing in this manner do takes come as the flies are being lifted off to recast. This is because the rising downstream movement is entirely natural and exactly how the real nymphs behave.

As with all fly fishing, the ideal presentation of the flies should be made into water no slower than that the floating line is resting on. Otherwise the fly line will move faster than the flies and quickly cause them to drag or speed up. If the intervening currents are faster than the fishing zone, line mending is essential until such time that the flies and line are drifting at the same pace. Whilst line mending is going on, the end of the line and fishing zone must remain monitored for takes.

Sometimes much is made of where on a three fly cast a particular pattern must be placed. There are no fixed rules except that of general guidance. The more obvious nymph imitations should be on the point as these will have the greatest movement and be subject to the longest rise when the cast is fished out. Any weighted patterns should also go on the point because they will fish deepest. The middle dropper is less critical and will accommodate any except the heaviest pattern of the team. The top dropper invariably fishes the slowest and is nearest the surface so it is usually reserved for patterns that could be taken for emergers, a dishevelled blur of legs, wings, body and nymphal skin, or for a drowned dun or spinner, or a terrestrial. There may well be times when three spiders need to be fished close to the surface and these will fish well anywhere on a leader. The only guidance to be offered is to position any heavier pattern or a clear nymph imitation on the point.

MINOR TACTICS

I sometimes fish a dry fly with a spider pattern on a single dropper. In doing so I'm hedging my bets and increasing my chances of success. In my experience no patterns are better than the Partridge and Orange or the Waterhen Bloa for such a tactic. The former seems to work throughout the season without any obvious answer as what it is taken for; the second is a fine general olive imitation, one species of which could be expected for eight or nine months a year. When fishing in such a way I fish as though I'm using only the dry fly and concentrate on the floating fly. Because my line of sight generally follows the leader to the fly I can see any subsurface swirls to the dropper or movement of the leader and react accordingly. Others may find it easier to concentrate on the dropper because the takes to the floating fly will be more obvious.

The other variation on this is to fish a nymph imitation on the dropper and I have enjoyed success with this too but mainly in moderately paced and faster water. Fishing this way on the Tweed a few seasons ago I enjoyed some excellent grayling fishing on local association water. From the middle of a shoal of grayling the dropper nymph hooked what I hoped was my biggest grayling ever; only a true thymallophile would have been disappointed to discover instead a sea trout of a couple of pounds.

At the Dutch Fly Fair I watched Theo Bakelaar tying some unusual grayling flies and my interest was immediately awakened as to whether his patterns would work for me. He ties two mini-leadhead nymphs in colours of proven success for grayling. One is based on the Red Tag and the other in the colours of the Imp, one of Rolt's favoured dressings. Both have a very small split-shot head painted black. These two patterns, known as the Green Last Hope and Black Last Hope have both caught grayling for me in the one late summer and autumn that I have tried them. It is not an extensive trial but they proved their value in catching grayling. They provide a way of getting a more traditional dressing deep. The additional aspect of the lead head has its own advantages. The black version has a body of dubbed CDC fibres. Theo maintains that air bubbles are trapped within the fibres, some of which are released as the fly is moved through the water. I have successfully fished the flies singly on a leader in the traditional nymph manner and as the point fly on a three fly leader. The additional weight ensures they fish deeper than the usual wet patterns. There may be other patterns which can be adapted by the inclusion of a very small split-shot.

One unusual grayling pattern that has come to light in recent years, but which has been spared the glare of publicity, is the imitation trout or salmon egg. Grayling feed on eggs when they are caught up in the drift and even weeks after spawning, well away from the redds, they will still respond to the imitation. It is not without good reason that some of the biggest grayling are caught in the best salmon rivers where high protein eggs become available at a time of the year when other food sources are scarce. I have been experimenting with weighted coloured beads and more conventional egg patterns achieving moderate success, but I need to do more work on their presentation and the timing and location of their use before passing more detailed comment. Part of their use involves discovering where and when trout or salmon spawn and finding the grayling downstream. Great care should be taken so that no spawning fish are disturbed or their redds destroyed. I believe there is scope for development of egg imitating patterns and fishing styles.

In his excellent book *Chalkstream Chronicle*, Neil Patterson describes the use of a Glo-Bug yarn egg pattern on autumn grayling in the Kennet. It is a pattern and method that has brought him considerable success with fish in the shallows and to three feet deep. I have not fished in this way to chalk stream grayling but I will summarise his method. It involves fishing very close to a shoal and unusually, keeping the fly line off the surface.

A small split-shot is pinched on the line about four inches above the egg. From a position directly across from the shoal cast a short line upstream so that the egg bounces along the gravel bottom. The rod tip is held high so that there is a direct line from the tip to the egg without any line floating on the surface. A twelve to fourteen feet leader is used with, in Neil Patterson's set-up, a hollow, tangerine-coloured, floating Shockgum section, four inches below the leader butt. The tip of the fly line or the Shockgum section should hang just above the surface and act as the indicator of the take.

When I use an egg pattern it is fished in a conventional upstream or across the stream style with the takes monitored in the usual way, with or without a bite indicator. I have not presented the egg with the line held clear of the surface unless when very close to the fishing zone. I have also used weighted beads without the need for the additional weight on the leader.

The egg patterns and fishing styles have yet to be fully developed for grayling. I suspect that its potential as a pattern will not be exploited fully until it is fished in the critical post-spawning period downstream of the trout or salmon redds.

The most successful fly fisherman will be the one prepared to observe, learn and adapt to the circumstances of the river, day by day, from one hour to the next, or even minute by minute. The nature of grayling is that they require no predetermined ideas about the patterns and fishing methods because they will change their feeding behaviour throughout the day. I fancy that chalk stream grayling are rather more predictable than those elsewhere, but my cautionary note is that it is often the most inexperienced grayling angler who is the most dogmatic or who will confidently predict success. The thoughtful angler will observe and adapt to maximise his chances of success; all that is required is a share of good luck.

Perhaps the modern angler, along with many other aspects of his life, is unduly preoccupied with statistics, or with success rather than enjoyment. Whether it is catch returns, numbers caught, sizes, growth rates, fish surveys of rivers, or autopsies of stomach contents, we are impressed when statistics prove or support our theories or validate our successes and excuse our failures. I am as guilty as anyone. I keep accurate records of each fishing day, recording weather, natural flies seen, successful artificial patterns and fish catches. Too often I find myself summarising my fishing day in terms of *x* grayling and *y* trout, or recording their weights as if these signify the pleasure or joy of the occasion. What I am apt to forget, but I hope I shall never lose sight of, is that the essential enchantment of fly fishing is quite independent of statistics.

6

Grayling Flies

THE MAJORITY OF RIVER trout flies catch grayling, after all they are imitating the same flies that both fish eat. Consequently, this chapter could warrant an entire book. I have omitted most of the specific imitations of natural flies unless there is something new about them or mentioned elsewhere in the book, or peculiarly of interest to grayling. Patterns for these natural flies can be found in good fly dictionaries. This fly list is by no means exhaustive but my selection is made because of personal experience or through the recommendation of other, very experienced grayling anglers and I hope reflects the trends in grayling fly fishing. It is also prepared for British grayling, which it seems feed fairly similarly to foreign grayling. Nevertheless, there are quite endless lists of French, German, Austrian, Danish, Slovenian, Finnish, Polish, Swedish, Norwegian, Czech, Canadian, Alaskan, Russian and Mongolian grayling flies of passing interest only for most anglers. I hope I will be excused for omitting all but those I have had highly recommended or have worked well for me or my friends. Never refuse local advice when fishing abroad or on an unfamiliar river, and if a Gold-headed Red-tagged Klinkhamer is what does the business in the feeder streams of the Sea of Tranquility, then simply ask what size you should tie them on.

I make no apology for featuring some of the most effective patterns from Oliver Edwards who has a very wide experience of grayling fishing. His credentials as a tier are plainly visible and are second to no-one's. What many fewer fly fishers will appreciate, unless they are fortunate enough to fish with Oliver, is that his flies are not just show pieces but are for fishing. Additionally, his reading of a river and fly fishing skills are unequalled. If it became necessary to have a single word to describe the extraction of grayling by fly, the name Edwards would be its root.

CADDIS

Caddis Larvae

All these are suitable for any of the deep nymph techniques and particularly the Eastern European short nymph methods.

Blackhead Caddis

A very simple pattern of mine that achieves depth very quickly. The black head does not detract from the dressing the way brighter beads may do on clear water. This is a good pattern for more wary fish.

Hook: 12 heavy wire or longshank 14–16

Thread: Black

Body: Mixed rabbit fur spun in a dubbing loop wound over an optional lead wire underbody

Thorax (on longshank version only): Wound cream or pale yellow wool

Rib: Fine gold or copper wire

Head: Black tungsten bead

Caseless Caddis (Hans van Klinken)

I have caught a lot of grayling from a wide range of rivers on this excellent pattern. The cream-coloured version is my favourite.

Hook: Partridge GRS12ST or K12ST (long shank emerger hook) size 12

Thread: Black

Underbody: Wound lead wire, a single layer at the abdomen, two layers at the thorax

Rib: Nylon mono, 0.2 mm, 12 wraps over the back

Abdomen: Dirty yellow, cream-coloured or olive green Furry Foam

Back: Transparent grey Flexibody strip over the abdomen and thorax

Thorax: Fitch (polecat) or dark brown mink spun in a dubbing loop and wound on, with guard hairs well picked out for legs after ribbing

Head: Black thread

Czech Nymphs

I am grateful for Oliver Edwards' personal comments to me about the dressing of these patterns. Those illustrated are tied by Oliver and are typical of his choice. An essential element in the dressing is the attainment of a rapid penetration to achieve depth quickly, and a slim profile, despite being well loaded with lead. They have no legs, hackles, etc, to hinder their descent. Traditionally, square-section lead is used which increases the mass considerably over round lead wire as the corners are filled in. However, the same results can be achieved by using a narrow strip of sticky-backed lead sheet. Tungsten wire is now available (Roman Moser Products) which is thin, very hard and springy, so requires supergluing at each layer. Its great advantage is that it is twice as heavy as lead.

There is no build up at the thorax and there is an abrupt taper at the head and abdomen. The dubbing is fine to medium coarse. There is no standard colour, but olives, greys, greens, pale or dirty yellow, hare's ear, etc, all work well. The Czech tying of including a very small 'hot spot' (orange, red, bright yellow) on the back of the thorax area is worth including. The thorax is about a quarter to a third of the total body length and can be any natural fur dubbing of a dark shade. Some of the guard hairs should be picked out.

Hook: Any curved grub type size 6–12

Thread: 6/0 or 8/0 to colour match the dubbing

Weight: Fine square lead (see text), keep slim and smooth

Abdomen: Fine or medium dubbing (see text) applied fine but must obliterate any sign of the lead

Hot Spot (Optional): One or two turns of bright orange or red dubbing

Thorax: Any spiky natural dark fur, hare, rabbit or squirrel, etc

Rib: Gold wire, fine flat gold tinsel, fine pearly, seven to nine turns

Shellback: Thin natural latex, 4 mm wide stretched over the back

Over Rib: 3 lbs b.s. mono, number of turns to match the dubbing rib

Head: Tinted black or brown with a Pantone pen

High Viz Czech Nymph (Oliver Edwards)

This was an accidental tying which has proved first rate in 'beery' Dales rivers running off. It is very visible in these conditions and grayling seem to prefer it to other Czech nymphs on the same leader. The dressing is as above but the abdomen is a pale yellowish-olive with a bright orange hot spot. The thorax is tan hare's mask fur plus the guard hairs and over-ribbed with fine gold holographic tinsel. The head is Pantoned light brown.

Finnish Cased Caddis (Veli Autti)

The example illustrated is tied by Oliver Edwards who praises it as having proved to be 'an exceptional pattern when used with the short line nymphing style, particularly for larger grayling'.

Hook: Long shank d/e size 6–12

Thread: White Roman Moser Powersilk

Weight: Narrow strips of sticky backed lead sheet wound over the 'case' area – the amount depending on the depth and flow to be fished

Case: Feather fibre cut (not stripped) from any large quill feather, colour to suit the natural cases. The fibre is rolled and crushed in the palm of the hand then teased out to form a long, loose roll. This is inserted into a dubbing loop and spun tight, then wound with touching turns over the lead for two-thirds to three-quarters of the shank. Finally, sculpt to shape, leaving it slightly rough.

Grub: White, cream or very pale green nylon knitting wool

Legs: Three pairs, golden pheasant centre tail fibres (see Hydropsyche larva)

Thorax marks (Optional): Narrow strip of brown polythene sheet or brown feather slip tied down twice as the legs are tied in. Alternatively mark with a Pantone pen. On completion give the entire larva, case and grub, a thorough coating with *very thin* head cement.

Hatching Sedge Pupa (Oliver Edwards)

The Raffene wing case (well soaked in water) is tied in before the thorax, then the thorax is dubbed and the Raffene looped each side of the thorax. The butts of the pheasant tail fibres are wrapped as a head.

Hook: Partridge K4A size 12–14

Abdomen: Light-green poly dubbing

Abdomen back: Dark green-dyed swan shoulder fibres ribbed with fine gold wire

Wing cases: A loop of dark brown or near black Raffene either side of the thorax

Thorax: Sepia and brown seal's fur

Legs and head: Cock pheasant tail fibres crumpled for effect

Antennae: Wood-duck or dyed mallard breast fibres

Hydropsyche Larva (Improved) (Oliver Edwards)

This a refinement of the dressing given in Oliver's book. He describes it as one of his 'must' grayling patterns.

Hook: Any curved grub hook size 8–12

Thread: 6/0 or 8/0 or Roman Moser Powersilk, white or olive

Weight: A narrow strip of sticky backed lead sheet, slightly fatter at the thorax

Tail Appendages (Optional): Dun coloured filoplume (aftershaft) from any game bird body feather. After tying in, the centre is stripped out forming a V, this is then shortened to about 2–3 mm

Abdomen and thorax: Soft 4 ply sparkle yarn, colour very pale olive, pale grey, or greenish olive (tint with Pantone pen if necessary), twisted very slightly

Legs: Six stripped fibres from a golden pheasant centre tail quill. Use the stripped hooked ends as the legs. Arrange in pairs at approximately 45 degrees on the underside.

Shellback: Brownish-olive Flexibody 3–4 mm wide with a tapered end

Rib: 3–4 lbs b.s. clear mono to follow the hollows of the corded abdomen and thorax

Gills: Brush out sparkle yarn fibres (The barrel cleaning brush for a 0.177 air rifle is ideal, claims Oliver)

Tinting: Black Pantone pen on the first three or four thoracic segments on the Flexibody

Rhyacophila Larva (Oliver Edwards)

Hook: Partridge K4A, size 8–12

Thread: Fine and strong, typically yellow Kevlar

Weight: Narrow strip of wine bottle lead in one or two layers

Abdomen and thorax: 4-ply knitting yarn, 100% synthetic fibre, or synthetic and natural blend. Preferably with the addition of Antron, or other highly reflective 'sparkle' fibre. Colour bright mid green. Take out 1 ply and use 3 ply only.

Rib: Clear or dyed green mono between 3–5 lb b.s., or a single strand of green Flashabou or a double strand of Datam Glo-Brite fluorescent floss, yellow shade 10

Legs: Partridge grey hackle barbs dyed yellow-olive

Upper abdomen tint: Medium olive waterproof felt pen. First three segments dotted with black waterproof felt pen

Head: Yellow thread or tint yellow if using white thread, sealed with Dave's Flexament

Rhyacophila Larva (Outstretched) (Oliver Edwards)

This represents the larva when it is lashing its body in a distressed or swimming mode. Oliver finds it a useful alternative to the popular grub or curved attitude.

Hook: Partridge Correct Attitude nymph H1B/CA olive coated

Thread: Green or olive

Weight: As for standard pattern

Abdomen and thorax: Bright mid-green to pale olive-green soft 4 ply sparkle yarn

Legs: As standard pattern

Shellback: Medium olive Flexibody

Rib: As standard pattern

Gills: Pick out small tuft of sparkle yarn at both sides of each segment along full length of the abdomen, trim to about 1.5 mm with scissors

Tint: Light brown Pantone pen on the tops of the first three or four segments

Leadhead Nymph

In a dead drift this is taken for a cased caddis and despite its size is taken by grayling. The lead or lead-substitute shot is crimped onto a piece of strong mono and bound onto the shank with the split towards the eye.

Hook: Partridge H1A or G3A size 8–14

Thread: Black or brown

Tail: Brown partridge tail fibres, partridge back fibres or a mottled soft wing feather from a hen pheasant, wound as a collar between the butt and the body; one or two turns only as the butt must show through

Butt: Fluorescent green Flexibody or fluorescent lime-green wool

Body: Shaggy brown rabbit fur, in a dubbing loop and wound

Head: Lead-substitute shot

Peeping Caddis

This is a series of cased caddis designs from the inventive vice of Oliver Edwards. All have the caddis grub imitation peeping out of the case. The grub is made from synthetic knitting yarn such as cream, yellow, olive-yellow or similar Antron or SparkleYarn in suitable Oliver Edwards Masterclass shades. A match flame is held to the end of the yarn. The fibres will fuse and turn dark brown. This will represent the head of the larva. It is tied in at the rear of the shank after the weight has been tied in over the eye. Other versions include different cases, such as tightly spun and packed deer hair which is trimmed to shape and soaked with highly thinned Flexament.

Hook: 2X or 3X long shank heavy wire size 6–14

Thread: Brown Kevlar or similar

Weight: Lead substitute shot nipped onto strong mono and bound to the shank

Case: Rabbit or hare's mask fur or mixed, with guard hairs, heavily applied and tightly dubbed with a dubbing whirl. When the fly is finished the body is roughed up with some Velcro and clipped to a circular, tapered case.

Legs: Brown or grey partridge hackle or dyed black, fairly short in the flue

Head: Antron yarn

Peeping Caddis (Crystal River)

This variation on the original Edwards dressing is available commercially from Crystal River, two of whose specialities are fluorescent and luminous materials. The latter are highly visible in the failing dusk if subjected to torch light before fishing. The differences from the original dressing are the weighted shot painted dark green and the larva represented by a luminous plastic bead which is attached by enclosing it in a fine stocking mesh.

Hot Head Caddis (Crystal River)

Hook: Long shank 10–12

Underbody: Lead foil or wire

Case: Mixed natural fur and hair and synthetic fibres, trimmed to shape

Legs: Brown partridge

Head: Vivid green oval Caddis Hot Head (Crystal River-Firefly) with a piece of mono through. The end is melted to seal it and provide a dark contrast

Silver Sparkle Bottom Caddis Pupa

This is a Roman Moser pattern for imitating the caddis pupa as it begins its ascent to the surface. The silver Kystal Hair imitates the translucent sheath around the natural pupa. It also works as a general deep pattern rather like a more reflective Killer Bug.

Hook: Partridge CS27GRS size12–16

Thread: Dark brown 6/0

Underbody: Double layer of lead wire over a drop of Superglue

Body: Dubbed medium-grey carpet wool mixed with some silver Krystal Hair, wound from the front with a second layer finishing at the eye. The fly is finished by roughing the body with a piece of Velcro.

Swimming Caddis Pupa

In devising this pattern, Roman Moser tried to copy the success of the gold-heads on the bottom with a pupa imitation nearer the surface. After experimenting with other body colours he was aware that orange was the preferred choice. The finished fly is fluffed up with a piece of Velcro.

Hook: Partridge CS27GRS size 10–18

Thread: Yellow 6/0

Abdomen: Orange carpet wool mixed with some SLF fibres for the sparkle effect

Legs: Two turns of light brown cock hackle, 2nd or 3rd grade. The lower fibres are trimmed away.

Thorax: Golden yellow SLF, tied fairly bulky

Superpupa

This is one of the patterns that proves the rule that the most effective patterns are often the simplest to tie. I have fished this very widely both during sedge hatches and as a general emerger imitation on the top dropper and it has become one of my most successful flies for grayling and trout. I vary the colours to match the naturals but the cream and brown version is my best. It is fished damp in the film or as a floater. I have experimented with a palmered CDC version but it hasn't matched the results of the original.

Hook: 12–18

Abdomen: Cream, olive or grey fine poly dubbing (Fly-Rite) along two-thirds of the shank

Thorax: Dark brown or black fine poly dubbing

Body hackle: Palmered cock: light brown on the cream body, blue-dun on the others, with the upper and lower fibres cut away

CDC Pupa (Leon Links)

This is another good summer late evening pattern, fished either dry or damp.

Hook: TMC 103 BL size 4–18

Body: Mixed olive and yellow Irise dub, or any other suitable coloured dubbing

Hackle: About six natural or dyed CDC feathers spun in a dubbing loop (the longer fibres towards the bottom) wound forward from half way along the body

Hackle: Palmered cul de canard feather

Klinkhamer Special

The fly from Hans van Klinken that changed grayling fishing irrevocably. Originally the hooks specified were Partridge code K12ST or GRS12ST. If these are used, whilst in the vice, the hook should be given an additional bend just behind the thorax before tying on it. Partridge now produce a pre-bent Klinkhamer hook code GRS15ST. I will quote Hans'[1] own tying instructions. 'After winding on the thread well round towards the barb, tie in the wing and fully secure along the shank with the thread. Tie in the hackle and then dub a slim tapered body, stopping behind the wing. Tie in three peacock herls and wind three turns behind the wing with three further turns in front. Tie off and secure with varnish. Turn the hook in the vice 45 degrees to face downwards. Wrap a base of Spiderweb at the base of the wing. Wind the hackle and secure the hackle tip between the wing and the body with half-hitches or a whip finish. Secure with varnish.' I tie the fly without tilting the hook at 45 degrees. The abdomen material is usually Fly-Rite poly dubbing but feather herls ribbed with wire can be used. Black feather fibre versions are very successful.

I often use a black mini Klinkhamer when grayling are taking smuts, midges or emerging very small black sedges which are very common from midsummer onwards on northern rivers. In this instance the hook should be a size 18 Partridge K4A or a fine wire equivalent. The body is wound black thread with a black hackle and a small stub of white wing.

Hook: Partridge GRS12ST or K12ST size 8–22

Thread: Sparton Micro grey for the body; Danville's Spiderweb for the base of the wing and tying in the hackle

Abdomen: Fly-Rite light tan poly dubbing, or dark tan or rusty olive

Wing: White poly yarn

Thorax: Three strands of peacock herl

Hackle: Blue dun (preferred), chestnut brown or light ginger cock. The author invariably uses natural red cock.

[1] *The World's Best Trout Flies* 1994 edited by John Roberts, chapter by Hans van Klinken

Little Red Sedge (G.E.M. Skues)

A very reliable general sedge imitation and search pattern.

Hook: 14–15

Thread: Hot orange

Body: Darkest hare's fur with a palmered short-fibred red cock hackle

Rib: Fine gold wire

Wing: Landrail wing, bunched and rolled and sloping well back over the body

Hackle: Five or six turns of dark red cock in front of the wings (longer-fibred than the body hackle)

Little Red Sedge (R.A. Stephens)

R.A. (Taff) Stephens has this very easy to tie pattern based originally on Skues' dressing. The result is a Red Palmer. This thin, wingless, anorexic fly might not appeal but in Taff's hands it caught eighty six Avon grayling in a mere two hours fishing.

Hook: 14–16 Partridge E1A

Body: Red tying silk wound the full length of the shank

Hackle: Palmered natural cock leaving the body very visible

Taff Stephens also has two winged variations with which he has caught very many grayling. He has a three pounds fourteen ounces Wiltshire grayling to his credit. The first is the Hirwen Sedge which has a wing of hen pheasant wing clipped in line with the bend and tied in after the upper body fibres are trimmed flat. His Tedge is a barred teal winged version.

Silhouette Caddis

Finnish angler, Juha Vainio has produced this excellent dry imitation. It has a number of features to copy the characteristics of the newly emerged adult: a lighter body colour and a translucent wing. The latter provides a translucent halo effect when viewed from below and is very suggestive of the emerging adult. It also fishes low in the film. The wing material is scarce in the UK but well worth experimenting with.

Hook: Tiemco TMC 2302 size 10–14

Thread: Yellow 8/0

Body: Yellow Antron dubbing

Body hackle: Short-fibred sandy dun cock with the upper fibres cut away before the wing is tied in

Rib: Fine gold wire

Wing: Snowshoe hare foot fur, not too dense

Thorax: Antron/Hare blend to suit

Head hackle: Dark blue dun cock, wound sparsely over the thorax

Squirrel Sedge (Lars-Åke Olsson)

This is an excellent riffle and fast water fly for bringing grayling to the surface. Lars believes in offering fish something to make the journey worthwhile. The wing, which is doubled and folded back over the body contains a lot of air, so when the body sinks, the fly still floats well. It was devised for Scandinavian grayling where the sedges are bigger and more prolific but the smaller sizes are useful in the UK.

Hook: Partridge E1A long shank 10–16

Thread: Brown

Body: Reddish brown summer red squirrel fur (substitute is hare's ear or mask fur) spun on a spinning block

Hackle: Natural red cock palmered with the upper fibres cut away and the lower section with a 'V' cut out

Wing: Reddish-brown squirrel tail, tied in behind the eye, roots behind the hook bend and points in front of the eye and then folded backwards over the first part of the wing. Make a big head of the upper part of the wing and whip-finish behind the head

Voljc Sedge

This style of winging a sedge is named after Slovenian, Dr Bozidar Voljc who devised this unique method of producing very durable and realistic sedge wings. The patterns should be varied in size and colour to match the naturals. The method of making the wings is thus[2]: a stocking mesh is spread tight in a frame and various game bird feathers are glued to the mesh underside down so that the shiny side of the feather is uppermost. The feathers are then cut out singly and trimmed to shape.

Hook: 12–16

Body: Palmered cock over the tying thread with the upper fibres cut away

Wing: Game bird feather, prepared as above, in a tight V, extending beyond the body

Hackle: Suitably coloured cock

Popa Caddis (Post Ovipositing Adult Caddis)

Whether the traditional winged wet sedge patterns have been taken for egg-laying females is debatable. However, I think Oliver Edwards is the first British tier to devise a pattern to represent specifically those species that swim to the stream bed to oviposit. I have seen how, in Oliver's hands, this catches a lot of grayling and trout as dusk falls in summer and sedges begin their egg-laying. Once they have deposited their eggs the females attempt to swim back to the surface. The Rhyacophilidae and Hydropsychedae species common on many grayling rivers exhibit this behaviour.

Hook: 10–16 curved sedge Partridge K4A

Thread: Olive or brown 8/0

Underbody (optional): A small amount of lead foil

Abdomen: Fine synthetic dubbing to match the natural or SLF on the larger sizes

Rib: Fine gold wire

[2] It is described in detail in *Oliver Edwards' Flytyers Masterclass*

Thorax and legs: Mixed chopped deer and elk hair with legs picked out and rear sloping

Wing: Raffene, doubled and then folded to produce four wings about 3–4 mm wide and extending about one and a half times the shank length, and trimmed to shape

Antennae (optional): Any dark animal hair with a fine tip

Head: Tying thread

NYMPHS AND BUGS

Bronze Nymph

This simple cased caddis imitation is a favourite of Jurek Kowalski's for the short nymph method. It is easy to tie and offers strong contrasting colours as a target in the deeper water.

Hook: Partridge G3A 8–10

Thread: Black

Underbody: Lead wire

Body: Wound dark brown wool ribbed with fine copper wire

Thorax: Wound yellow wool

Hackle: Brown hen

Head: Tying thread tied large

Dove Bug

I first mentioned this bug of mine in the original edition of *The Grayling Angler* when there had been very few bug patterns devised for fishing deep. It has brought me a lot of success and to many other anglers too. My biggest British grayling of two pounds six ounces fell to this. If an even faster sinking rate is required I tie a version with a copper bead head. I prefer the version with a copper underbody; I think it catches more fish because of the lighter colour visible through the translucent dubbing. It is important to mix the colours of the dubbing and not have a single colour.

Hook: 10–12

Thread: Brown

Body: Underbody of copper or lead wire. Seal's fur – natural cream and olive, mixed equally with a pinch of red with the fibres picked out

Rib: Fine gold tinsel, copper wire or mother-of-pearl Crystal Hair

Faisan and Orange

The original of this bug was devised by Frenchman Raymond Rocher. The version described below is as amended by Robert Spiller and has been a consistently reliable grayling pattern.

Hook: 12

Thread: Black

Underbody: Fine copper or lead wire

Tail and back: Cock pheasant tail fibres

Body: Orange suede chenille ribbed with gold wire

Gold-head Pheasant Tail Nymph

A number of variations of Sawyer's original nymph have been evolved with the main purpose of getting a small, slim nymph even deeper. I prefer the copper bead version as its colour is more in keeping with the rest of the materials. I do very well with it in fast shallow water or as an alternative to a bug when grayling are growing wary. Most of the variations are similar to each other with a colour change at the thorax or with a gold, copper, silver or black bead-head. Some have a wing case of cock pheasant tail fibres over the bead, others do not. I very much like my olive version which has a tiny olive hen hackle between the short olive thorax and the copper bead.

Hook: 10–16 standard or slightly long shank

Thread: Brown

Tail: Cock pheasant tail fibres

Underbody (optional): A small hump of wound copper wire at the thorax

Abdomen: Cock pheasant tail fibres ribbed with fine copper wire

Thorax: Natural or dyed fur; rabbit, hare or squirrel

Head: Copper, gold, silver or black bead, 2 or 3 mm depending upon hook size

Chatsworth Bug

Devised by Robert Spiller for Derbyshire grayling and trout. It is similar to many other nondescript gold-head bugs ideal for achieving depth quickly.

Hook: 10–14 standard or long shank

Thread: Brown

Tail: Six short strands of pearl Krystalflash

Body: Pine squirrel body fur ribbed with gold wire

Collar (optional): Green or orange fluorescent dubbing

Head: Gold bead

Copper Head Seal's Fur Bug

A bead-headed version of the Dove Bug which is typical of many similar bugs.

Hook: 12–14 Partridge E1A or MM2A

Underbody (optional) Wound copper wire

Back: Four strands of mother-of pearl Crystal Hair

Body: Mixed yellow, orange and olive seal's fur

Rib: Copper wire wound over the back

Head: 4 mm copper bead

Copper Squirrel

Another of my own grayling and trout bugs which includes a hackle for additional mobility.

Hook: 12–14

Body: Grey squirrel fur in a dubbing loop ribbed with fine gold tinsel or wire

Brown partridge tied behind the bead

Head: Copper bead 4 mm

Goldbead Peacock Runner (Theo Bakelaar)

Hook: Tiemco TMC 3761 size 10–12

Thread: Brown

Bead: 4 mm gold bead

Tail: Two widely spaced goose biots

Body: Five or six peacock herls twisted together with the thread

Legs: Two goose biots tied in at the side at the rear of the thorax and tied rear facing

Thorax: Six peacock herls wound together with the thread

Gold Ribbed Hare's Ear

This general emerger imitation passes for a number of dun species struggling in the process of breaking through the surface film. It can be tied with a coloured bead to fish deep or alternatively on longer hooks with a lead wire underbody to imitate a cased caddis. However it is used, it is as successful as it is versatile, whether floating or bumping along the bottom.

Hook: To suit, from a longshank 12 to standard 18

Tail (only on the floater, and then optional): A few long body strands

Underbody: Lead wire, only on the version to be fished deep

Body: Hare's ear ribbed flat gold tinsel

Legs: Long body fibres picked out, on the floater only

Grey Goose Nymph

This is Frank Sawyer's imitation of the nymphs of the pale wateries and spurwings. It is tied in the same manner as his Pheasant Tail nymph, without the aid of tying thread, by winding the herls and the copper wire together.

Hook: 12–16

Tail: Tips of the grey goose fibres

Body: Grey goose wing fibres and golden-coloured copper wire wound together over a layer of copper wire. Additional weighting is achieved by a copper wire thorax underbody

Thorax: Body fibres doubled and redoubled and tied in with the copper wire

Heptagenid Nymph (Oliver Edwards)

Hook: Partridge H1A size 16–18, or E1A size 14–18

Thread: Danville's Spider Web

Weight: Narrow strip of wine bottle lead foil or fine copper wire

Tails: Pale moose mane hairs dyed pale yellow-olive, or any pale, stout, quick-tapering animal hair, dyed yellow-olive.

Abdomen: Thick polythene (0.2 mm) dyed yellow-olive, or yellow-olive Flexibody

Under abdomen tint (optional): Brown waterproof felt pen on the dorsal side; fluorescent yellow on the ventral side

Abdomen gills: Ostrich herl dyed yellow-olive

Thorax and head capsule: Golden-yellow fine synthetic dubbing (SLF Finesse Masterclass MC6)

Head capsule cover: Brown Raffene

Legs: Guinea fowl undercovert or flank hackle dyed yellow-olive, coated with flexible cement and re-coated after heat-kinking to shape

Wing buds: Dark, brick-red, red grouse hackle coated with cement or clear flexible adhesive

Killer Bug or Grayling Bug

Rarely has a fly been more aptly named than Frank Sawyer's answer to the problem of overpopulation of grayling on a chalk stream. Although today we have a much wider choice of fly to achieve depth quickly it remains a very successful pattern, catching thousands of grayling each season both on chalk streams and elsewhere. This nondescript dressing passes for a shrimp or newly emerged sedge pupa. It is extremely easy to tie. Sawyer specified the original body wool as Chadwicks darning yarn, shade 477, now unavailable, but various beige shades work well. My preferred substitute is dubbed light tan Fly-Rite poly-seal. My own experience is that the version with a copper wire underbody outfishes the one with a lead wire underbody. The copper shines through the translucent wet wool in a more attractive fashion than lead. Other variations have evolved. My friend, Roy Shaw, has even had success with an all black version; perhaps the Kiwi Bug? I have added a copper ball and a partridge hackle to the standard Killer Bug to include the aspects of mobility and brightness to the dressing. It certainly works well, to the extent of over eighty grayling in a few hours from Sawyer's home river, but whether this would have been better than the original, who can say?

Hook: 10–14

Thread: None

Underbody: Layers of lead or copper wire in a cigar shape

Overbody: Wound beige darning wool tied in with fine copper wire

Last Hope

When Theo Bakelaar first showed me these mini Leadheads I knew that here were two unusual patterns for achieving a moderate depth with a small fly in proven grayling colours. Any imparted movement of the fly by the angler means that the fly moves in attractive undulating wiggle. Its creator suggests that the cul de canard version retains air bubbles around its fibres which are released as the fly is given short, sharp movements.

Hook: Long shank 16–18

Head: Small lead or substitute split shot bound in on mono and painted black

Tag: Red wool or yarn

Body: Peacock sword herl for the green version; black CDC fibres (without the quill) or CDC dubbing twisted on to copper wire (010 mm) for the black version

Little White Head Nymph

Adam Sikora is a Polish International angler, twice the runner-up in the World Championships, on one occasion coming second on the Welsh Dee where he caught a lot of his grayling on this pattern using the short nymph techniques. Adam suggests that it works well in a dead drift but sometimes requires some slight control across the current. It was devised by Franciszek Szajnik.

Hook: Tiemco TMC 100 size 10

Thread: Pale beige

Underbody: Lead wire

Abdomen: Rust or copper-coloured wool ribbed with red copper wire

Thorax: Cream-coloured wool

Pheasant Tail Nymph

There is no better general nymph imitation on the chalk streams than Frank Sawyer's. It represents all the agile-darting species. It is usually fished to visible fish and worked in the induced-take style. Its moderate sinking rate allows it to be fished a couple of feet or so below the surface and its imparted movement and slim profile complete the deception.

Hook: 12–16

Thread: None originally but it is eaier to tie with brown thread

Tail: Three cock pheasant tail fibres

Underbody: Copper wire with a hump for the thorax

Overbody: Pheasant tail fibres wound on with the copper wire and tied fatter at the thorax

Wing case: Pheasant tail fibres doubled and redoubled

Pink Nymph

This is a sort of Polish Killer Bug recommended by Adam Sikora for grayling throughout the season but having its best results in autumn and winter. It is important that the colour of the wool should be preserved when wet. To aid this, Adam uses an underlayer of synthetic plastic tape.

Hook: Tiemco TMC 2302 size 8–12

Thread: Black

Underbody: Lead wire

Body: Pale orange-pink wool

Rib: Gold wire

Head: Varnished black thread

SHRIMPS

Shrimp (Phil White)

Hook: 10–16

Underbody: Lead wire or several slips of lead foil built up on top of the shank

Back: Brown Raffene, not prestretched, to overlap both sides

Rib: Fine gold or copper wire wound over the back

Body: Mixture of medium olive and hot orange seal's fur in varying proportions, with the longer fibres picked out for legs

Edwards Shrimp (Oliver Edwards)

Hook: 10–14

Thread: Grey

Underbody: Lead wire or foil in a hump on top of the shank

Tail and head appendages: Pale olive-dyed or natural grey partridge fibres

Back: Clear polythene

Body: Dubbed mixture of very pale olive-dyed fur and grey partridge hackles, picked out for legs

Rib: Nylon mono over the back

Red Spot Shrimp (Neil Patterson)

The red spot on the natural shrimp is nearer orange than on this dressing so it may be worth experimenting with the spot colour.

Hook: Curved 8–14

Thread: Waxed olive

Underbody: Fine lead wire

Body: A short length of fluorescent red wool is tied on in the centre of the shank, at a right angle to it; then an equal mixture of olive mohair and olive seal's fur is dubbed and wound on. The red wool is clipped to form a spot on each body side

Back: Double layer of clear polythene over the rib

Rib: Gold wire

Legs: Body fibres picked out

Orange Bead Shrimp (John Roberts)

I have enjoyed some remarkable catches with this pattern. Sometimes I have used it when other shrimps or the Killer Bug were achieving modest success but on turning to this the takes increased by a few hundred percent. The bead may appear glaringly bright to the angler, but for grayling I believe it is a definite trigger.

Hook: Partridge K4A size 12

Thread: Tan

Bead: 3 or 4 mm fluoresecent orange plastic bead (Firefly – Crystal River)

Underbody: Two separate lead or copper wire humps either side of the bead

Body: Dubbed tan Fly-Rite poly-seal

Back: Clear polythene

Rib: Copper wire over the back

Shrug

This is Simon Ashworth's very successful grayling bug, a combination of shrimp and Killer Bug. The body wool is teased into individual fibres and then dubbed, not wound.

Hook: 12–14 Kamasan B100 or Partridge K4

Underbody: One or two layers of lead wire

Body: Beige darning wool (original Chadwicks 477) with the fibres picked out through the ribbing

Rib: Glo-Brite neon magenta floss

Back: Clear olive or colourless polythene overribbed with fine gold wire

Woven Nymph

This is one of many woven nymph types fished in the Eastern European style on a short line. Variations can be tied in other colours. Most are tied in natural shades but lately I have seen brighter colours used. This example is tied by Polish nymph expert Adam Sikora who fishes this style very widely for grayling

Hook: Tiemco TMC 2302 size 6–12

Flyfishing for grayling on the River Test.

Top: A twenty-inch (51cm) grayling acrobatically performs on the River Gim in Sweden.

Left: The clear limestone waters of the Slovenian river Idrica reveal this
flyfisher's excellent grayling

Above: A beautiful Canadian grayling, in the author's experience slightly browner in their body colour than British fish and the dorsal fin has strong blue tinges. Below: Oliver Edwards, master of all subsurface styles, watches the end of his fly line for signs of a fish. Grayling in fast water allow a careful angler to approach very closely.

Summer fishing on the West Beck. Oliver Edwards is the successful angler.
Below: Autumn grayling fishing amidst jungle terrain of the River Wylye

Top; A large male grayling over the spawning beds of the River Aare, Switzerland. Below: A grayling rise to the natural fly on the surface of the tributary of the River Aare.

Top: The frenzy of spawning; one hen spawns with a male but is immediately joined by two cock fish which shed their milt over the same eggs.
Below: A grayling at the head of about thirty brown trout. The grayling is first in the feeding order on this Swiss river. In the author's experience big grayling are not ousted from their lies by trout and will often be caught in the prime feeding positions.

Top: A nymph's eye view of three grayling actively feeding in the Inn River of the Swiss Alps.
Below: Cased caddis with the larvae protruding prominently – a favourite grayling food. In some areas of the river bed there may be hundreds per square metre.

Top: Chalk stream grayling have a habit of shoaling between weed beds. In this picture they mull about in the slow flow, some maintain their position near the bottom, others more actively cruise the pool. Below: Sedge pupae: all taken by a grayling as they ascended to the surface for emergence.

Top left, in descending order:
Sparkle Aphid (Links).
CDC Aphid (Davison).
Mini Black Klinkhamer.
Once & Away. Gold Ribbed Hare's Ear.
F Fly. Culard.
Masham Midge.

Top right, left to right descending:
Sika Deer Hair Sedge (Links). Klinkhamer Special. Sparkle Caddis (Weaver). Squirrel Sedge (Olsson). Silhouette Caddis. Little Red Sedge.
Balloon Sedge. F Sedge.

Left, left to right descending:
Spent Willow (Edwards). Spent Spinner (Roberts). Lacoste. Naked John Storey. Gim River Dun. Pale Watery Paradun (Roberts). Terry's Terror.
Sparkle Emerger (Weaver).
Olive Paradun (Roberts). Sturdy's Fancy.
Janus.

Left, left to right descending:
Three Czech Nymphs (Edwards).
Caseless Caddis (van Klinken).
Rhyacophila Larva (Edwards).
Woven Nymph (Sikora).
Pink Nymph. Bronze Nymph.

Left, descending:
Hydropsyche Larva (Edwards).
Hot Head Caddis.
Peeking Caddis (Edwards).
Extended Rhyacophila Larva (Edwards).
Leadhead Nymph (van Klinken).
Finnish Cased Caddis (Veli Autti).

Left, descending from left to right:
Bradshaw's Fancy. Grayling Witch.
Rolt's Witch. La Peute.
Orange Bumble.
Honey-Dun Bumble. Light Watchet.
Poult Bloa. Snipe & Purple.
Partridge & Orange. Waterhen Bloa.
Black Spider (Olsson). Fog Black.
Dark Watchet.

Below left, descending:
Green Last Hope.
Glo-Bug Egg. Killer Beetle.
Black Last Hope.
Five Piam Nymphs.

Below, descending:
Heptagenid Nymph (Edwards).
Copperhead Pheasant Tail Nymph.
Blackhead Pheasant Tail Nymph.
Sawyer's Pheasant Tail Nymph.
Grey Goose Nymph.

Descending from left to right:
Copper Squirrel. Copperhead Killer Bug.
Killer Bug. Faisan & Orange (Spiller).
Shrimp (White). Shrimp (Edwards).
Dove Bug. Shrug.
Copperhead Seal's Fur Bug. Goldhead Hare's Ear.
Orange Spot Shrimp.

Descending:
Superpupa.
Moser Pupa.
CDC Pupa (Links).
Silver Sparkle Bottom Pupa.
Ascending Sedge Pupa (Edwards).
Popa Caddis.

Thread: Black

Underbody: Lead wire

Body: Plaited synthetic fibres; viscose or floss silk; the upper fibres dark grey, the lower white

Wingcase: Black hen fibres coated with clear varnish

Rib: Black thread wound over the wingcase

Head: Black thread

NORTH COUNTRY SPIDERS

All North Country spider patterns should be tied with short bodies, typically ending in a line midway between the point and the barb or occasionally as short as in line with the point. All should be sparsely dubbed and wound with a maximum of a couple of turns of hackle only. The hackle should be tied in by the tip. The hackle fibre length extends back to just beyond the bend.

Dark Watchet (Edmonds & Lee)

Mainly used when the iron blues are hatching and a good general grayling fly.

Hook: 14

Body: Orange and purple tying silks twisted together and finely dubbed with mole's fur

Hackle: Jackdaw's throat feather

Fog Black

One of Pritt's favourites as a top dropper, this is a reliable fly throughout the year. Drowned small black terrestrials regularly appear in grayling diets and the imitation is worth using throughout the season.

Hook: 12–14

Body: Dark purple silk or thread

Rib: Magpie or ostrich herl

Wing: Starling wing quill as a substitute for the original bullfinch

Hackle: Starling neck feather

Needle-fly or Brown Owl

Hook: 14

Body: Orange silk

Hackle: Reddish or dark feather from the outside of a brown owl's wing

Head: Peacock herl

Partridge and Orange

If my choice of North Country pattern was restricted to just one, either for trout or grayling, this would be the one. Like all the most successful patterns it represents whatever fish want to see in it, whether a mature stonefly or blue winged olive nymph, or a drowned adult aquatic fly. It is usually fished on the middle dropper. Below is the Edmonds and Lee version which specifies the Pearsalls silk shade. The 6A shade originally specified is different today and is not the strong chestnut orange required.

Hook: Size 14–16, typically Partridge L3A

Body: Orange silk, Pearsalls Gossamer, optionally ribbed with gold wire or tinsel

Hackle: Brown mottled feather from a partridge back or neck

Head: Orange silk

Poult Bloa

One of the best imitations to use when pale wateries and spurwings are hatching.

Hook: 14–16

Body: Yellow or primrose tying silk with an optional very sparse dubbing of natural red or ginger fur

Hackle: Slate-blue feather from a young grouse underwing

Snipe and Purple or Dark Snipe

Traditionally an iron blue dun imitation I have caught a lot of October grayling with this most unimpressive looking fly. Oliver Edwards will fish it is as small as a size 20 when it also imitates some of the small dark terrestrials.

Hook: 16–18, typically Partridge L3A

Body: Purple silk Pearsalls No.8

Hackle: Dark feather from the marginal coverts of a snipe's wing

Head: Purple silk

Starling Bloa

A superb grayling fly for when the small spurwings are emerging.

Hook: 18–20, typically Partridge L3A

Body: Straw-coloured or white silk

Hackle: Undercover feather from a young starling's wing

Waterhen Bloa

Although this is most effective early season for the large dark olives it also fishes well in October and November when a second emergence period is common. I will use it throughout the summer whenever fish are taking olives in the film or just below the surface. It is one of the patterns that every North Country trout and grayling angler uses. The body should be very sparsely dubbed so that the tying silk is clearly visible through the fur. There are slight variations in the dressing. This is the Edmonds and Lee version.

Hook: Size 14–16, typically a Partridge L3A

Body: Yellow silk (Pearsalls Gossamer No.4) dubbed with mole's fur

Hackle: The inside of a moorhen's wing, the smoky-grey feather from the under coverts (the darker side of the feather towards the eye)

Head: Yellow silk

Winter Brown

A needle fly dressing based on Pritt's version.

Hook: 14

Thread: Orange silk

Hackle: Inside of a woodcock's wing

Head: Peacock herl

GENERAL DRY FLIES

Adams

This North American fly is one of the most popular trout flies across the world. It also is a good grayling fly. The Parachute Adams is even better.

Hook: 14–16

Thread: Grey

Tail: Grizzle hackle fibres

Body: Dubbed blue-grey wool or fur

Wings: Two grizzle hackle tips tied upright

Hackle: Red and grizzle cock wound together

Parachute Adams

Hook: 12–20

Thread: Grey

Tail: Light or medium blue-dun cock fibres

Body: Dubbed grey muskrat fur

Wing: White poly yarn or calf tail, tied upright

Hackle: A grizzle and natural red cock wound together round the base of the wing.

Badger Series

These traditional grayling flies are fished wet or dry and have in common the badger hackle. The Double Badger is the one I have most success with. The Green Badger and Blue Badger are the same as the Red Badger except for an appropriate body colour.

Double Badger

Hook: 14–18

Body: Peacock herl

Hackle: Badger cock at each end of the body in the fore and aft style. The rear hackle is sometimes smaller than the front

Red Badger

Hook: 14–18

Body: Red floss tipped with silver tinsel

Rib: Silver wire wound through the hackle

Hackle: Palmered badger cock or hen

Silver Badger

Hook: 14–18

Tag: Red wool or poly yarn

Body: Flat silver tinsel ribbed with oval silver through the hackle

Hackle: Palmered badger cock or hen

Head: Red wool or poly yarn tag

Black Jack

A pattern I have used for nearly twenty five years for grayling taking small dark flies from the surface.

Hook: 16–18

Body: Brown seal's fur

Wing: Two small wings of dyed hackle fibres, one bright red, the other yellow or light green, set slanting rearwards at about 45 degrees and shorter than the hackle

Hackle: Black cock

Bumbles

The Bumbles, which can be fished wet or dry, are really two series of flies, one originating in Derbyshire and of untraceable ancestry, such is their age; the others were popularised by Halford and were primarily dry flies. All have a palmered hen or cock hackle, and in the case of the Halford patterns, all have a rib of peacock herl. Quite what they are taken for, I can only guess but many grayling fishers swear by them and the Orange and Pearly versions have been highly recommended.

Furnace Bumble

Hook: 12–14

Body: Orange floss

Rib: Peacock sword herl

Hackle: Palmered furnace cock or hen

Honey-Dun Bumble

Hook: 14–16

Body: Salmon-pink floss

Rib: Peacock sword herl

Hackle: Palmered honey-dun cock or hen

Orange Bumble

Hook: 14–16

Body: Orange floss

Rib: Peacock sword herl and fine gold wire or tinsel

Hackle: Palmered honey-dun over front half of the body

Collar Hackle: Slightly longer body hackle

Pearly Bumble (Adrian Jones)

Hook: 12–14

Thread: Brown or olive

Tail: Olive hackle fibres

Body: Pearl Lurex ribbed with olive-dyed grizzle

Rib: Silver wire

Collar Hackle: Slightly longer body hackle

Steel-Blue Bumble

Hook: 14

Body: Alternate bands of orange, light-orange and cherry-coloured floss silk

Rib: Peacock sword herl

Hackle: Steely-blue hen or cock

CDC Magic

A German pattern from Gerhard Laible which has been highly recommended for British and Continental grayling. The original was tied with a white CDC wing but a black or very dark grey wing has been more successful in the U.K.

Hook: 16–20

Tails: Four Microfibbets in two bunches spread apart

Body: Fly-Rite extra fine poly dubbing to match the natural

Wing: Two or three CDC plumes set upright with the body fibres dubbed over the wing roots

Coachman

The Grayling Coachman differs from the standard dressing below by a red wool tag and an alternative wing of white hackle fibres or poly yarn slanting over the body or set upright.

Hook: 14–16

Thread: Black

Body: Bronze peacock herl

Wing: White duck or swan fibres

Hackle: Natural light-red cock

Culard

This small dark nondescript fly from Hans van Klinken is an excellent midge, smut or small terrestrial imitation to be fished in the film or wholly dry. The black-bodied version is preferred for grayling.

Hook: Long shank 16–18

Thread: Black

Body: Herl fibres from a black peacock wing feather or dark grey or blue-dun synthetic dubbing

Rib: Extra-fine gold wire or yellow silk

Wing: Four cul de canard feathers pulled together and cut half-way along the body length

Hackle: Two turns of very small dark blue-dun cock (dry) or a starling body feather (emerger)

The F Fly

Marjan Fratnik rediscovered the use of cul de canard feathers and in 1983 produced the F Fly around which many other patterns have been devised. By altering the body colour and size, a wide range of duns, midges and smuts can be represented. When grayling want low-riding imitations in the film these are excellent.

Hook: 12–22

Body: Originally coloured tying thread or very sparse muskrat fur, or any fine dubbing

Hackle and wing: One small cul de canard feather for size 18–22; two small feathers for size 16; three for size 12, trimmed to shape

A variation on the F Fly theme comes from John Davison, for many years editor of the *Grayling Society Journal* who ties an unnamed green CDC fly, a very good grayling pattern and I would imagine a fair aphid imitation. In the absence of a name John suggested C-de Vert but I prefer his pithy Yorkshire 'a little green un'.

Hook: 20–22

Thread: Dark green micro

Body: Fluorescent green thread

Wing: Cul de canard clipped level with the bend

Gimriver Dun

Lars-Åke Olsson devised his series of dun imitations taking the best of what he saw in other styles: the split tails, the Catskill style of the hackle placed towards the middle of the body either side of the wing, the V cut into the lower hackles to aid its more natural support on the surface. The fly invariably lands correctly and stands very like the natural dun. It is a very accurate style which Lars has used on many rivers, from the chalk streams and spring creeks to the Madison and big Swedish rivers. The colours of the materials and size should match the natural. The Green Gimriver Dun is described.

Hook: Tiemco TMC 103 BL size 13–19

Thread: Olive

Tail: 4 Microfibetts, in two 45 degree groups

Wing: A single bunch of male mallard mottled breast fibres

Body: Olive-green dyed natural fur

Hackle: Blue dun cock with a 'V' clipped in the underside, wound over the thorax

Grayling Fiddler

A fly from Eric Horsfall Turner for grayling taking tiny surface flies.

Hook: 18

Body: Brown tying thread taken round the bend just short of the barb and lightly dubbed with red wool

Hackle: Small grizzle cock

Grayling Steel Blue

One of Roger Woolley's excellent patterns which may be fished either wet or dry.

Hook: 14

Tip: Three turns of orange tying thread with a tiny tip of silver tinsel

Body: Bronze peacock herl tied slim ribbed with gold wire

Hackle: Grizzled bright-blue dun cock, palmered

Grey Duster

An excellent general dry fly for use throughout the summer and autumn. I prefer the parachute version but many other anglers hold the standard dressing in very high regard.

Hook: 12–18

Tail (optional) Badger cock fibres

Body: Blue-grey rabbit's fur

Hackle: Badger cock

Griffith's Gnat

An American trout fly which works well for smutting grayling. One August I took an American guest to the Ure which was suffering with very low water. Grayling were dimpling on the surface in eighteen inches of a nearly motionless flow. My friend had caught half a dozen grayling, his first ever, on a size 24 Griffith's Gnat before I had even moved one.

Hook: 16–26 fine wire

Thread: Black micro

Body: Peacock herl

Hackle: Very short-fibred grizzle palmered along the body

Hare's Ear

When grayling are rising to tiny flies on a slow unrippled surface the simple Hare's Ear will often work very well. It is so nondescript grayling see in it whatever they are looking for. The trick is to tie it as scruffy as possible, with fibres sticking out everywhere, and to fish it on a fine sunken leader point.

Hook: 16–22 fine wire

Thread: Pale yellow

Body: Hare's ear fur

Rib: Finest gold tinsel or wire

Janus

This pattern in the fore-and-aft design was created by Dr Hal Thirlaway of the Piscatorial Society. I am grateful to Robin Mulholland for pointing out to me its virtues. The head hackle should be shorter-fibred than would normally be used.

Hook: 20–22 fine wire

Body: Black thread tied slim

Tails/wing: Four long grizzle fibres tied at about 55 degrees to the rear, fanned

Rear hackle: Natural dark red cock

Shoulder hackle: Short-fibred badger, grizzle or white cock

John Storey

This is a fine North Country general dry fly originally tied for the River Rye, one of the most beautiful grayling rivers in the country and one that produces very high quality grayling. Sadly, there is no access now for the visiting angler.

Hook: 14 down-eye

Thread: Black

Body: Copper peacock herl

Wing: A small whole mallard breast feather tied in a sloping bunch forward over the eye

Hackle: Dark red cock

John Titmouse

Eric Horsfall Turner devised this grayling variant of the John Storey for when grayling were proving difficult to hook on a small dry fly. He believed this fly improved his success rate and two hundred grayling fell to it in its first season's use.

Hook: 16–18

Thread: Black

Tail: White hackle fibres

Body: Peacock herl

Wing: Very small mallard breast feather, about 8 mm long, sloping forward over the eye

Hackle: Black cock

Lacoste

This rather unusual design was recommended to me by the Belgian grayling angler, Hugo Martel who came across it in Austria and has used it for some years on rivers all over Europe. It is possibly taken for an aphid or perhaps an emerging midge.

Hook: 12–18

Body: Green silk taken round the bend of the hook

Thorax: Peacock herl tied short

Hackle: Grizzle cock with the tips coloured brown with a waterproof felt pen

Masham Midge

My own answer to the problem of grayling taking tiny surface flies.

Hook: 18–22

Thread: Grey micro

Body: Chocolate-brown Fly-Rite poly dubbing

Hackle: Blue-dun cock, optionally with the lower trimmed level with the body

Naked John Storey

I like the idea behind the concept and naming of this very underdressed John Storey devised by John Woods. It fishes as an emerger with the body hanging vertically, supported by the collar hackle in the film. The wing is highly visible to the angler. John has had a lot of success with it for grayling, particularly the orange version.

Hook: Fine wire 14–20

Body: Stripped peacock herl, natural or dyed orange, red or olive

Hackle: High quality natural red cock

Wing: Mallard breast fibres bunched and forward-sloping

Norman's Fancy

I liked the look of this fly the moment I saw it. It was devised by R.A. (Taff) Stephens and named after Norman Smith, keeper of the Wilton Fly Fishing Club on the Wylye. I have used it successfully a number of times over a recent short period. The variegated multicoloured body is highly unusual and is produced by winding an unnamed multistranded natural yarn obtained from a haberdashers. This may be very difficult to reproduce but I've no doubt that a similar material will work. I prefer to trim the lower hackles so that the body is flat on the surface.

Hook: 14–16

Body: Multistranded, multicoloured yarn (ginger, white, maroon, olive and dark blue)

Hackle: Badger cock

Once and Away

This is a general emerger pattern from Hans van Klinken. In my experience it works best in its small sizes for dimpling grayling taking the invisible tiny smuts, midges or terrestrials from the film.

Hook: Partridge GRS12ST 18–22, given a further downward bend

Thread: Fine black

Body: One peccary fibre or any stripped quill as a substitute taken well round the bend

Thorax: Peacock herl

Wing and wing case: Six or seven cul de canard feathers, secured in the upright position; place a tiny drop of varnish at the base, avoiding the rump fibres; trim to a tuft

Orange Otter

This well known grayling fly comes recommended by other anglers. I have caught grayling on it, but not many. There are plenty of other anglers who do far better than me with it.

Hook: 12–16

Tail: Natural red cock fibres

Body: Mixed hot orange and claret seal's fur 3:1 (otter substitute) tied in 2 halves

Hackle: Natural red cock in the middle of the body

Paradun

My preference for the parachute style of dry fly has resulted in two paraduns to imitate most of the duns I encounter. The first is a general olive imitation, which copies all the olives by just a slight change in body shade and hook size. I use the second pattern for the lighter duns, the species grouped as pale wateries, so common throughout the late summer and early autumn.

Olive Paradun

Hook: 14–22

Thread: Sparton Micro olive

Tail (optional): Microfibbets widely spaced or a few Z-lon fibres

Body: Fine olive Fly-Rite poly dubbing

Wing: Upright white or grey poly yarn (siliconised yarn from Niche Products is the best)

Hackle: Blue dun or natural red cock wound round the wing base

Pale Watery Paradun

Perhaps the most exceptional catch I've had on this is the seventy to eighty Avon grayling which couldn't resist it over the course of a single afternoon. The dressing is as for the olive version except that the body is pale yellowy-beige Fly-Rite poly dubbing and the hackle is blue dun or ginger cock.

Pepper's Own

This is a fine general dry fly from Tony Pepper devised for his native Yorkshire rivers.

Hook: 14–16

Thread: Purple

Tail: Three strands of cock pheasant centre tail herls tied to twice the body length

Body: Wound cock pheasant tail herls

Rib: Red silk

Hackle: Red cock with a honey grizzle nearest the eye

Red Spinner (John Roberts)

My favourite spinner imitation for late summer evening fishing.

Hook: 14–18

Thread: Red

Tails: Widely spaced Microfibbets

Body: Stripped dyed red peacock quill or any very fine red translucent plastic ribbing material

Wing: Magic Spinner wing fibres or substitute tied spent

Thorax: Thinly dubbed fine brown poly dubbing wound over the wing roots

Red Tag

With a century and a half of proven success for grayling no-one should overlook the humble Red Tag. It is fished either wet or dry. There are other versions, namely the Green, White and Crimson which have appropriately coloured tags. The Gold Tag has a tip of gold tinsel.

Hook: 12–18

Tag: Scarlet or bright red wool or poly yarn

Body: Bronze peacock herl

Hackle: Natural red cock or hen

Roger's Fancy

In his day, Roger Woolley was an expert grayling fisher and a fly dresser for over sixty years, much of that time as a professional. This is one of his favourite grayling flies.

Hook: 14–16

Tail: Red floss

Body: Pale blue heron herl

Rib: Silver wire

Hackle: Pale blue hen

Head: Short red floss sloping forward over the eye

Rusty Spinner (Mike Weaver)

Hook: 16

Tail: Microfibbets or 4 fibres of slate-grey cock hackle, divided in two bunches by a small ball of dubbing

Body: Dubbed rusty-orange fine fur with a thorax wound round the wing roots

Wings: Grey poly yarn tied spent

Sparkle Dun

An American pattern devised by Craig Mathews and John Juracek, it has proved very successful for John Goddard for grayling. It represents a stillborn dun with the nymphal shuck still trailing from the abdomen.

Hook: 16–20

Thread: To match the body colour

Shuck: Single strand of Z-lon between a half to one body length

Body: Fine natural or synthetic fur to match the natural's colour

Wing: Spun deer hair (ideally from the side of the neck or upper leg from a western whitetail deer) in a 180 degrees, comparadun style

Sparkle Emerger

Mike Weaver ties this emerger on the Sparkle Dun theme. It is excellent for grayling requiring a low-lying dry fly.

Hook: 12–20

Tail: White poly yarn, Z-lon or Antron body wool

Body: Dubbed natural fur or substitute, one-third in front of the wing

Wing: Natural or dyed deer hair; the wing is shorter than for the dun and slopes back over the body

Spent Willow and Needle Fly

Oliver Edwards ties this very impressive looking imitation for those warm October days the naturals find their way onto the grayling menu. When preparing the wings, the Raffene should be dipped into very thinned Flexament and allowed to dry, and then repeated. An alternative stronger wing material is Stalcup's Medallion Sheeting marketed by Umpqua. The fly illustrated is tied with the mottled brown type.

Hook: 16–20

Thread: Danville's Spider Web, tinted dark brown with a waterproof felt pen

Abdomen: Stripped peacock eye quill tied slim

Legs: Dark red or dyed very dark olive brown hen tied in at the rear of the thorax and wound over the thorax and wings

Thorax: Very dark olive brown fine synthetic dubbing in a small thorax

Wings: Two slips of Brown Raffene (see text), tied in so that each slip ties two wings on the same side of the body, or Stalcup's Medallion Sheeting

Antennae: Brown guard hairs from a mink tail or similar

Sturdy's Fancy

A Yorkshire grayling pattern with a national reputation. It is best fished dry and is a fair spinner imitation. I prefer the parachute hackled version.

Hook: 14–20

Tag: Red wool or poly yarn

Body: Bronze peacock herl (sometimes ribbed with red silk)

Hackle: White or creamy cock or hen at the shoulder or in parachute style

Treacle Parkin

This is a variation on the Red Tag to be fished either wet or dry. The difference in the dressing lies in the wool tag which is either yellow or orange. It is also a very good summer trout dry fly.

Universelle

I am grateful for Hugo Martel for drawing my attention to this Belgian pattern described in Dr J. P. Pequenot's book *French Fishing Flies*. It is primarily a sedge imitation and has been in use for almost seventy years. The tail appendages are inaccurate for a sedge unless they represent the trailing pupal sheath of a newly emerged adult or the dipped abdomen of an egg-layer. Hugo comments that it is a good all round fly and also effective in a Mayfly hatch when the wings of the duns are not fully erected.

Hook: 12–16

Tail: Pheasant wing fibres to match the wing

Body: Hare's face dubbing ribbed with yellow thread

Wings: Sections of cock or hen pheasant wing feathers

Hackle: Natural red cock

Witches

The Witches are a series of proven grayling patterns to be fished wet or dry. The following are the best two of the series.

Rolt's Witch

Hook: 14–16

Tag: Red floss

Body: Green peacock herl

Rib: Fine gold wire

Hackle: Palmered honey-dun

Grayling Witch (Roger Woolley)

Hook: 14–16

Tag: Red floss

Body: Green peacock herl

Rib: Silver wire

Hackle: Palmered blue-dun cock

TERRESTRIALS

Ants

It was not until recently that I had associated ant imitations with grayling. This most recent summer and autumn I followed the advice of others who had found them effective, and now after some perseverance I have joined their ranks. Hans van Klinken relates how he has fished large ants in northern Scandinavia as soon as the winter ice has melted and well before any natural ants could appear. Grayling took them readily, perhaps remembering their silhouette from the previous summer and associating it with surface feeding. The pre-made balsa wood bodies in the dressing below are from Orvis.

Hook: 14–18

Thread: Black

Body: Two small cylinders of balsa attached to each other by mono, varnished black, or black Plastozote foam

Hackle: Black cock trimmed top and bottom

Aphids

From midsummer to September aphids are often blown onto the river from nearby or overhanging trees. Grayling love them and a good imitation can be very successful.

Sometimes any small green fly will work but I like a pattern that emphasises a short bright green body. In addition to the dressing below, see under the F Fly.

Hook: 16–22 fine wire

Body: Lime-green floss wound, or dubbed lime-green poly yarn in a short body

Hackle: Short-fibred light blue dun, optionally with the lower hackles trimmed flat

Green Insect

A reliable summer pattern for fishing wet or dry.

Hook: 16

Tag: Red wool, yarn or floss

Body: Bright green peacock herl

Hackle: Small grey or blue dun cock or hen

Killer Beetle

This is Peter Welsh's wet imitation, usually fished on a trailing tippet behind a dry fly or deep behind a bead head.

Hook: 14–16

Thread: Black

Butt: Killer bug yarn

Underbody: Wound lead wire

Body: Peacock herl

MISCELLANEOUS

Black Spider (Lars-Åke Olsson)

Small black aquatic and terrestrial flies feature in grayling diets throughout the year. This small wet fly is a useful addition on a three fly leader.

Hook: 16–22

Thread: Black

Shoulder: A small knob of black or dark brown fur or peacock herl behind the hackle

Hackle: Black-green metallic neck or shoulder feather from a starling, or a black hen as a second choice

Bradshaw's Fancy

Reg Righyni included this as the point fly on his favourite three-fly cast for grayling.

Hook: 14–16

Thread: Purple

Tag: Crimson wool or floss

Body: Copper coloured peacock herl

Hackle: Norwegian or hooded crow (pale blue dun hen)

Head: Two turns of crimson wool or floss, or a forward slanting tag over the eye

Glo-Bug

Over the most recent season I have experimented with patterns to represent the eggs of trout, and where applicable, salmon. I was first alerted to the use of the imitation of the trout's eggs in Neil Patterson's excellent book *Chalkstream Chronicle*. This is his imitation.

Hook: 16

Thread: Orange monocord

Body: Five parts Cream Delight or Baby Pink Glo-Bug floss

Eye: One part Flame Glo-Bug floss

Hare's Ear Buzzer

This is Malcolm Greenhalgh's answer to the midge pupa on rivers. The manner of tying is unusual in that no tying thread is used.

Hook: Partridge L2A size 14–16

Thread: Finest copper wire

Body: Under thorax of copper wire, then take the wire to the end of the body and trap in a different coloured copper wire. Both are wound back to the thorax as a banded abdomen. Cut off the second wire.

Thorax: Hare's ear fur dubbed on the wire

Head: Two turns of wire and two half-hitches

La Peute

I am grateful for the recommendation by the distinguished fly fisher Marjan Fratnik of this old French wet fly. Literally 'the ugly', it was a very popular pattern twenty or thirty years ago, with a considerable reputation for difficult fish. Marjan has fished it extensively over recent seasons with excellent results. It looks to me as though it might be taken for a wide range of drowned duns or sedges.

Hook: 12–20

Body: Yellow tying thread

Hackle: Mallard hen breast feather trimmed flat 3 mm beyond the bend of the hook, no more than one and a half turn on size 16 and smaller, two turns on size 14 and larger

Priest

A useful wet fly for coloured water. A similar fly is Brunton's Fancy except that the front two-thirds of the body is green peacock herl. On this a cock hackle is used for a useful dry fly.

Hook: 14–16

Tag: Red ibis subs or red wool

Body: Flat silver tinsel

Rib: Oval silver wire

Hackle: Badger hen

Sage

Reg Righyni devised this wet fly which he hoped would pass for an egg-laying spinner. It has also caught salmon, by accident, and so its name, the Salmon Approved Grayling Enticer, arrived.

Hook: 14–16

Thread: Crimson

Tail: Orangey-yellow floss

Body: Mixed claret rabbit's fur and claret polar bear's fur

Rib: Fine gold tinsel

Hackle: Hooded crow or pale blue-dun hen

Appendix A

A List of the Grayling Rivers and Streams in the United Kingdom

The main river is listed first and its grayling-holding tributaries follow afterwards.

SCOTLAND

Tay – Tummel, Earn, Isla, Ericht, Dean, Kerbert, Alyth, Braan, Farn, Machany, Pow, Ruthven, Keithick Burn, Lunar Burn, Lyon, Shochie Burn

Almond

Clyde – Avon, Douglas Water, Mouse, Medwin N & S, Duneaton Water, Gryfe, Green Water, Lochar Burn, Culter Burn

Ayr – Lugar, Coyle, Greenock Water

Tweed – Kale, Jed, Till, Glen, Leet, Teviot, Breamish, Beaumont, Rule, Ede, Leader, Oxnam

Annan

Nith

Irvine

North Esk

ENGLAND AND WALES

Thames Water Authority

Thames – Evenlode, Windrush, Coln (Glos), Churn (Glos), Pang (Berks), Blackwater, Brain, Kennet, Kennet & Avon Canal, Lambourn (Berks), Dun (Berks), Aldbourne, Chelmer (Essex), Enbourne (Berks), Wey (Surrey/Hants), Tillingbourne (Surrey), Coln (Glos), Darent, Wandle, Lee, Charwell

Southern Water Authority

Itchen

Meon

Test – Wallop Brook, Anton, Pill Hill Brook, Golden Brook, Dever, Bourne, Blackwater, Dun, King's Somborne Brook

Medway – Eden

Stour (Kent)

Rother (W.Sussex), Lod

Broadlands Lake (Romsey)

Anglian Water Authority

Welland – Gwash

Witham

Great Eau or Withern – Ludd

Yare – Wensum

Lark (tributary of the Great Ouse), Ise, Chater

Wessex Water Authority

Bristol Avon – Chew, Marden

Hampshire Avon – Bourne, Wylye, Nadder, Ebble, Till

Frome (Dorset)

Piddle

Brue

Tone

Stour – Allen, Shreen

South West Water Authority

Exe – Batherm, Culm, Barle, Lowman, Brockey, Creedy, Haddeo

Tamar – Carey, Lyd, Inny, Kensey, Otter, Thrushel, Lew, Bolesbridge, Deer, Claw

Tone

Northumbrian Water Authority

Derwent

Blyth – Pont

Wear

Tees

Severn Trent Water Authority

Severn – Onny, Tanat, Banwy, Vyrnwy, Teme, Clun, Corve, Rea

Trent – Soar, Derwent, Wye, Lathkill, Dove, Bentley Brook, Churnet, Amber, Manifold, Anker, Blythe, Sence, Henmoor Broook, Churnet, Tean

Welsh Water Authority

Dee – Alwen, Lliw, Llyn Tegid (Lake Bala), Tryweryn, Twrch

Teifi

Wye – Monnow, Lugg, Arrow, Llynfi, Irfon, Ithon

North West Water Authority

Eden – Eamont, Lowther, Crowdundle Beck, Belah, Helm Beck, Hilton Beck, Hoff Beck, Irthing, Lyvennet, Leith, Scandal Beck, Trout beck

Ribble – Hodder

Dane (tributary of the Weaver)

Gowy

Yorkshire Water Authority

Esk

Ure – Cover, Skell, Laver

Wharfe – Skirfaire

Nidd and Gouthwaite Reservoir

Swale – Bedale Beck, Cod Beck, Wiske

Aire

Derwent – Rye, Thornton Beck, Seven, Dove, Riccall, Pickering Beck, Costa/Oxfolds Beck

Hull – Driffield Canal, Driffield Beck/West Beck

Appendix B

Grayling Growth Rates

The data below can be assumed in most cases to be a rough guideline only. This is because the number in the sample in some instances was fairly small, and in all instances no allowance was made for the difference in growth between the sexes. Studies by J. V. Woolland and J. W. Jones on grayling growth rates in Llyn Tegid and the River Dee indicate that changes occur in the length/weight relationship throughout the life of grayling. The general trend is one of increasing weight per unit length up to 3 or 4 years of age, followed by a decrease in subsequent years. There is no significant difference between the growth of the two sexes until sexual maturity in the third year when the males grow faster than the females.

Location	length (cm)						Number in sample
Age	1	2	3	4	5	6	
Upper Dee	12.0	21.3	27.0	31.6	33.4		1806
Dee (Corwen)	12.5	23.8	30.8	34.4			included in above
Llyn Tegid	12.0	22.5	29.8	35.8	37.9	39.9	2071
Lugg	11.0	16.7	26.0	30.3			unknown
Test	15.9	28.6	33.5	38.7	41.3	43.2	unknown
Itchen	14.9	24.7	29.9	35.3		90	
Dever	13.5	25.6	32.4	36.7	37.3	38.8	70
Anton	15.3	27.7	34.7	35.5	38.2	119	
West Beck (Driffield)	15.1	26.4	32.8	36.7	40.6	42.0	185
Ure		24.5	29.3	31.2			45
Wharfe	11.8	23.1	27.2	30.5	31.8		25

References for the above data.
Dee and Llyn Tegid: Woolland J.V. and Jones J.W. Studies on Grayling, *Thymallus thymallus* in Llyn Tegid and the upper Dee, North Wales. *J.Fish Biol* vol 7 1975
Lugg: Hellawell J.M. (1969) Age and determination of the grayling (*Thymallus thymallus*) of the Afon Llynfi and River Lugg. Ph.D. Thesis, University of Liverpool.
Test: Hutton J.A. (1923) Something about grayling scales. *Salm. Trout Mag.*
Itchen, Dever and Anton: Southern Water Authority
West Beck, Ure and Wharfe: Yorkshire Water Authority

The Grayling Society

The Grayling Society is a conservation body. It exists to promote all aspects of grayling and grayling fishing. I warmly commend the Society and its aims, and the camaraderie of its members to all grayling fishers not yet enlisted. The General Secretary is Steve Skuce, 7 Oaktree Way, Little Sandhurst, Berkshire GU47 8QS.

E-Mail: 101504,1312 @ Compuserve.com

Bibliography

Broughton, Ron, (editor), *Grayling, The Fourth Game Fish*, 1989

Carlstein, Mikael, *Feeding, Growth and Survival of European Grayling in Culture and after stocking*, Swedish University of Agricultural Sciences, 1996

Claypole, H.G.C., *Grayling: How to Catch Them*, 1957

Gardiner, Ross, *Scottish Grayling: History and Biology of the Populations*, SOFAD, 1992

Goddard, John, *Trout Flies of Britain and Europe*, 1991

Jackson, J., *The Practical Fly Fisher: More particularly for Grayling or umber*, 1854

Kite, Oliver, *Nymph Fishing in Practice*, 1963

Lake, R. And Woolley, R., *The Grayling*, 1946

Maclean, Norman, *Trout and Grayling, An Angler's Natural History*, 1979

Patterson, Neil, *Chalkstream Chronicle*, 1995

Platts, W. Carter, *Grayling Fishing*, 1939

Pritt, T.E., *The Book of the Grayling*, 1888

Righyni, Reg, *Grayling*, 1968

Roberts, John, *The Grayling Angler*, 1982

Roberts, John, *The World's Best Trout Flies*, 1994

Roberts, John, *Collins Illustrated Dictionary of Trout Flies*, 1995

Rolt, H.A., *Grayling Fishing in South Country Streams*, 1901

Sawyer, Frank, *Nymphs and the Trout*,1958, revised 1974

Walbran, F.M., *Grayling and how to catch them*, 1895

The newsletters and journals of the Grayling Society, 1977–1998